Royal London

Royal London

JANE STRUTHERS

Photography by

RICKY LEAVER

NEW HOLLAND

For my dear friends Stephen Cowin and
Stephen Rooke, with much love

First published in 2005 by New Holland
Publishers (UK) Ltd
London • Cape Town • Sydney • Auckland
www.newhollandpublishers.com

Garfield House, 86–88 Edgware Road,
    London W2 2EA, United Kingdom
80 McKenzie Street, Cape Town 8001,
    South Africa
14 Aquatic Drive, Frenchs Forest,
    NSW 2086, Australia
218 Lake Road, Northcote, Auckland,
    New Zealand

ISBN 1 84330 958 0

Publishing Manager: Jo Hemmings
Project Editors: Camilla MacWhannell, Rose
Hudson, Gareth Jones
Cover Design and Design concept: Alan
    Marshall
Designers: Paul Turner and Sue Pressley
Editor: Sarah Larter
Maps: William Smuts
Index: Angie Hipkin
Production: Joan Woodroffe

Reproduction by Pica Digital (Pte) Ltd,
    Singapore
Printed and bound by Kyodo Printing Co
(Singapore) Pte Ltd

CONTENTS

INTRODUCTION

It is impossible to separate London from its history. Every building, street, shop and statue has a story to tell about its past – whether it happened yesterday or 1,000 years ago. Sometimes part of the story is self-evident, perhaps because we are looking at a well-known palace, museum or monument, although, inevitably, there are tales about such subjects that we have yet to discover. Sometimes we may not realize the significance of what we are looking at – maybe because it has become dwarfed by its surroundings or its story has been forgotten over time – and we need to be reminded of its history.

It was my aim to bring these places to life by retelling some of the many incidents that took place in the city. This book reveals the royal links behind many places in London and the stories that are connected with them. These sites range from world-famous tourist attractions, such as Buckingham Palace, to places and objects that are less well-known but still have a royal significance, such as the York Watergate near the Strand and the Coronation Stone in Kingston-upon-Thames. As for the stories, they range from celebrated events that are a notable part of British history to interesting vignettes that give us a fascinating slant on the social life of the past.

Of course, there would be no royal history without the members of the Royal Family themselves, and it is these men and women who have made British history so colourful and vivid over the centuries. Some of these individuals, such as Henry VIII and Charles II, are larger than life, yet the stories about them in this book reveal them to be flesh and blood human beings, rather than cartoon characters or pantomime villains dragged from the pages of history. We feel for Henry VIII, who was informed that his fifth wife, Katherine Howard, was unfaithful to him on the very day that he attended a thanksgiving service for their

LEFT: *The Coronation Stone in Kingston-upon-Thames is said to have been used for the coronations of seven Anglo-Saxon kings.*

OPPOSITE: *Since 1066, every English coronation has taken place in Westminster Abbey, sometimes with dramatic consequences.*

marriage at Hampton Court. We can picture the 'Merry Monarch', Charles II, leaning over the wall that separates St James's Park from Pall Mall while he chatted to his mistress, Nell Gwyn, and probably eyed up other contenders for her position as they strolled past.

Sometimes, knowing about the events that took place in a famous building helps us to view it with fresh eyes. Instead of one of London's biggest tourist destinations, it becomes the setting for a dramatic or embarrassing incident that touched the lives of the people involved. For example, Westminster Abbey has seen many coronations over the centuries, but surely those ancient stones must have trembled at the coronation of George IV. Bewigged, powdered and draped in extravagant robes that he had designed himself, George was crowned while his estranged wife, Caroline, banged desperately on the doors of the abbey in a futile attempt to enter and take what she saw as her rightful place by his side as his queen. She was cheered by the watching crowds on her way to the abbey and booed by them on her way back. Who said there is anything new about royal scandal?

There are so many layers of history in London's streets and buildings that it is essential to be selective about what to include in a book like this. In this case, I have included items that still exist, even if what is left is only a fragment of an item's former glory. This means I have been able to include Richmond Palace, because part of its gatehouse is still standing, but have had to exclude other buildings that have long since vanished, such as Durham House, which played a minor but significant role in 16th-century royal history.

London is a huge, sprawling city so *Royal London* is divided into seven geographical sections. There is an inevitable concentration of royal sites in some areas of London, such as Mayfair, the Embankment, Whitehall and Greenwich, because these are places where members of royalty have lived for centuries. Other areas are less densely packed with places and objects of royal significance because there were fewer reasons for royal figures to visit them. Nevertheless, each area of London offers places of interest and, sometimes, intrigue, where the many members of British royalty can once again be remembered in the stories that are connected with them.

Jane Struthers

KEY TO MAP

WESTMINSTER
1. Constitution Hill
2. Buckingham Palace
3. The Queen's Gallery
4. The Royal Mews
5. The Guards' Museum
6. Birdcage Walk
7. St James's Park
8. Queen Victoria Memorial and Gardens
9. Green Park
10. Spencer House
11. Clarence House
12. St James's Palace
13. The Queen's Chapel
14. Marlborough House
15. Pall Mall
16. St James's Square
17. Waterloo Place
18. The Mall
19. Horse Guards Parade
20. The Banqueting House
21. Westminster Abbey
22. The Palace of Westminster
23. The Jewel Tower
24. St John's Smith Square
25. Bust of Charles I
26. Carlton House Terrace

THE CITY
27. St Bartholomew's Hospital
28. The Church of St Bartholomew-the-Great
29. Smithfield
30. Ireland Yard
31. St Paul's Cathedral
32. Queenhithe
33. Williamson's Tavern
34. The Church of St Mary-le-Bow
35. St Lawrence Jewry
36. The Guildhall
37. The Clockmakers' Company Museum
38. The Bank of England

39. The Royal Exchange
40. The Monument
41. London Bridge
42. The Tower of London
43. Statue of Queen Alexandra

Chapter 3

PICCADILLY TO HACKNEY
44. Queen Street
45. St James's Church
46. St Anne's Church
47. Soho Square
48. National Portrait Gallery
49. St Giles-in-the-Fields
50. Trafalgar Square
51. Statue of Charles I
52. St Martin-in-the-Fields
53. Statue of George III
54. Coutts & Co
55. Savoy Chapel
56. Bow Street Police Station
57. Theatre Royal, Drury Lane
58. Somerset House
59. St Mary le Strand
60. Temple Bar
61. Temple Church
62. Prince Henry's Room
63. St Dunstan's-in-the-West Church
64. St Bride's Church
65. York Watergate
66. Holborn Circus
67. Ely Place
68. Gray's Inn
69. German Hospital

MARBLE ARCH TO HIGHGATE
70. Marble Arch
71. Regent's Park
72. London Zoo
73. St Katharine's Chapel
74. St John's Wood Barracks
75. St George's Church
76. Queen Square
77. The British Library
78. Lauderdale House

WEST LONDON
79. Hyde Park
80. Hyde Park Corner
81. Mandarin Oriental Hotel, Hyde Park
82. Rotten Row
83. Eaton Square
84. The Royal Hospital
85. King's Road
86. Harrods
87. The Victoria and Albert Museum
88. The Science Museum
89. The Royal Albert Hall
90. The Albert Memorial
91. Kensington Gardens
92. Kensington Palace
93. St Mary Abbots Church

SOUTH-EAST LONDON
94. The Prince Consort's Model Lodge
95. Lambeth Palace
96. Greenwich Park
97. The Old Royal Naval College
98. The Old Royal Observatory
99. The Queen's House
100. Blackheath
101. Rotherhithe
102. Eltham Palace
103. The Royal Naval Dockyards and Arsenal

SOUTH-WEST LONDON
104. Royal Botanic Gardens
105. Kew Palace
106. Syon Park
107. Richmond Palace
108. Richmond Park
109. Orleans House Gallery
110. Bushy Park
111. The Coronation Stone
112. Hampton Court Palace

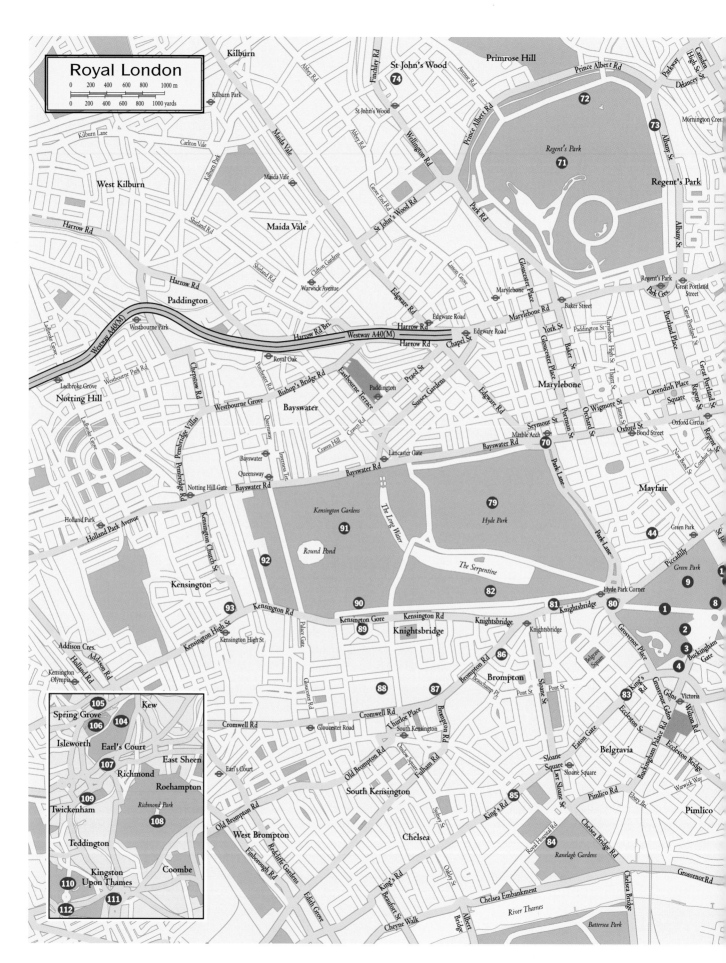

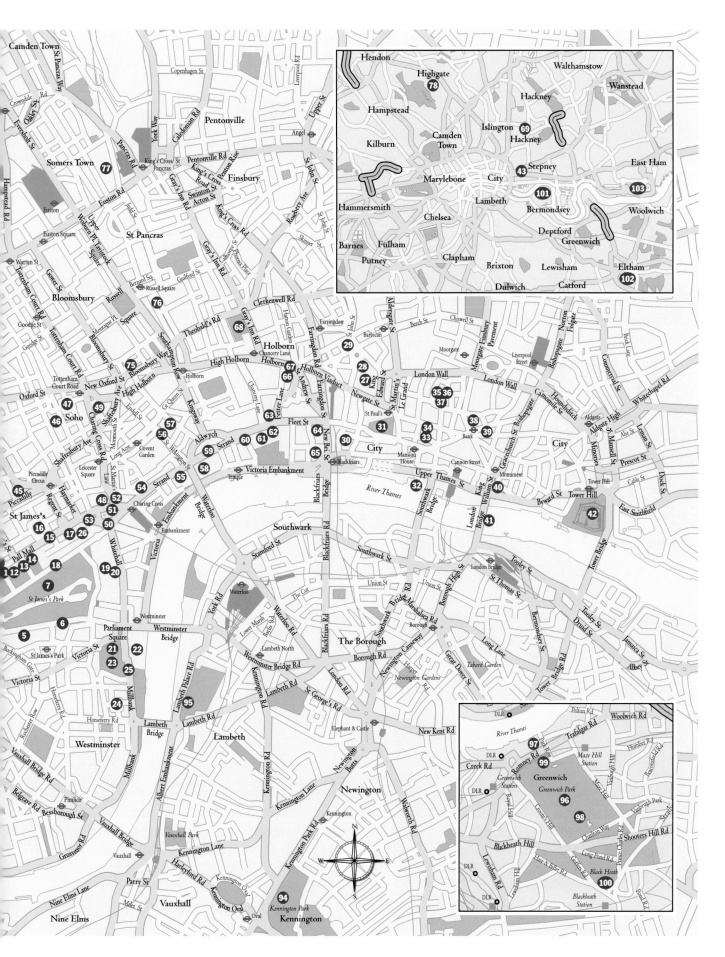

Chapter 1

WESTMINSTER

From the sumptuous interiors of Buckingham Palace to the site of James I's aviary in Birdcage Walk, Westminster is an area of London that is rich in places with royal connections. Some of these sites are world-famous, while others are treasures that are waiting to be discovered. They include the banqueting house of a medieval palace where Charles I lost his head, a tower in which Edward III kept his most valuable possessions and the royal park that was once the burial ground of a leper hospital.

LEFT: *The banners of the Knights of the Bath still hang above their stalls in Westminster Abbey.*

OPPOSITE: *The Guardsmen who stand outside Buckingham Palace are continuing a long tradition, but are also a big tourist attraction.*

CONSTITUTION HILL
SW1

To paraphrase Lady Bracknell in Oscar Wilde's play *The Importance of Being Earnest* (1895), to experience one assassination attempt along Constitution Hill may be regarded as a misfortune, but to experience three looks like carelessness. However, this is exactly what happened to Queen Victoria (1837–1901), whose life was threatened here in 1840, 1842 and 1849.

Strangely enough, she was not the only monarch whose life was thought to be in danger in Constitution Hill. Charles II (1660–85) enjoyed taking his constitutional walks along the road, which, it is believed, is how it got its name. One day his younger brother, James, Duke of York (1633–1701), was unnerved to see Charles strolling along the route with a very modest retinue of servants. He chastized his brother for taking such risks with his personal safety, to which Charles replied, 'I am sure no man in England will take away my life to make you king.' In the event, Charles was probably right. The Duke of York succeeded to the throne as James II in 1685, but his reign lasted just three years before he became so unpopular that he had to flee to France and a life in exile.

BUCKINGHAM PALACE
SW1

An aged mulberry tree grows in the grounds of Buckingham Palace, the solitary remnant of the vast walled garden of 10,000 black mulberry trees planted here in the early 17th century by James I (1603–25). He had high hopes of establishing a profitable silk industry, but he was obviously given bad advice, as the mulberry trees he chose were unpalatable to silkworms. The worms may not have cared for the trees, but the splendours of

the garden were extremely popular with Londoners, who used it for courtship among other pursuits.

In 1702, John Sheffield, the 1st Duke of Buckingham and Normanby (1648–1721) leased the land and commissioned William Winde to build him a house. Buckingham House was considered 'one of the great beauties of London' and, when the duke died in 1721, his widow offered it to the Prince of Wales, who later became George II (1727–60). Negotiations came to nothing but, in 1761, George III (1760–1820) bought the house for £28,000 from Buckingham's illegitimate son. He intended it to be a family house and, soon after, he gave it to Queen Charlotte (1744–1818) in exchange for Somerset House (see page 68), in which she had considered living. Buckingham House then became known as the Queen's House, and was extended in a manner fitting for the private residence of the monarch's consort. When Queen Charlotte died in 1818, her son, George, the Prince Regent (1762–1830), inherited the house. The building also had another change of name, becoming the King's House, Pimlico, in preparation for the prince's inevitable elevation to sovereign upon his father's death.

Nash and Blore

The builders moved in, but the renovations and improvements to the house failed to satisfy the Prince Regent who had begun to consider what to do with the royal palaces when he inherited them. By the time he became George IV in 1820 he had already decided that the King's House was far too small for him, and, after much wrangling with Parliament over the cost, he commissioned the architect John Nash (1752–1835) to build him a larger, more lavish palace. Naturally, this being the flamboyant George IV, the budget spiralled out of control and the palace became increasingly grandiose. It was still unfinished when he died in

ABOVE: *The royal coat of arms decorates the wrought-iron Forecourt Gates, which were created in 1914.*

OPPOSITE: *Buckingham Palace's Grand Staircase was designed by John Nash for George IV, and was made by Samuel Parker.*

1830, and his brother, William IV (1830–37), succeeded to the throne. Nash was sacked in 1831 for allowing the cost of the building to soar, which seems rather unfair, as preventing George IV from spending money was as impossible as making water flow uphill – both acts defy the laws of nature. However, the palace had to be completed, and

ABOVE: *The famous balcony on which the Royal Family appear during special occasions is above the arch on the East Front of Buckingham Palace.*

the architect Edward Blore (1787–1879) was given the task.

Here were two very different personalities from their respective predecessors. William IV was much more down-to-earth than George IV and had little interest in architecture. He had even less interest in Buckingham Palace, and suggested that it should be used as a barracks. However, the Prime Minister of the day, Charles Grey (1764–1845), persuaded William that this would be throwing good money after bad and that it made more sense to continue the original plan of turning Buckingham Palace into a royal residence. As for Edward Blore, he was seen as a safe – not to say pedestrian – pair of hands after the flights of fancy conjured up by John Nash; there was no danger of Blore spending hundreds of pounds on intricate plaster ceilings and marble columns. Instead, he was the man to get the job done and to do it as cheaply and unimaginatively as possible.

Victoria's Family Home

Despite Blore's best efforts, the palace was still in need of considerable work when Queen Victoria moved into it shortly after her accession in 1837. She and Prince Albert (1819–61), whom she married in 1840, lived with the builders for years while the palace was enlarged to transform it into a family home. The palace flourished until Albert's death, at which point Victoria retreated into mourning and the building was neglected.

By the time Victoria's son, Edward VII (1901–10), became king in 1901, the palace was a fusty relic of a bygone age and in need of considerable renovation. Since then, work has been carried out as necessary. In 1913, the east front of the palace was refaced in Portland stone, using money left over from the funds raised to build the Queen Victoria Memorial (see page 22).

Public View

For decades, the only way the public could visit Buckingham Palace was if they worked here, received a special invitation or were presented at court, as, for example, young debutantes were during the coming-out season. However, in 1993 the palace was opened to the general public for the very first time. This arrangement, which occurs while the Royal Family are on holiday at Balmoral in Scotland during August and September, has continued ever since. A total of 19 staterooms are now open to the public, including the Music Room, in which members of the current Royal Family, including Charles, Prince of Wales (born 1948), Anne, the Princess Royal (born 1950), Andrew, Duke of York (born 1960) and Prince William (born 1982), were all christened.

Twenty investitures take place in the ballroom of the palace each year, during which ordinary people and celebrities alike receive the honours that have been conferred on them by the Queen. There are also at least three garden parties within the palace grounds each year, following a tradition that began in the 1860s. Attendance is strictly by invitation only, with about 8,000 guests at each occasion looked after by about 400 staff. At each of these parties the staff provides about 27,000 cups of tea, 20,000 sandwiches and 20,000 slices of cake.

Buckingham Palace continues to be the pivot around which the British Royal Family is seen to revolve. It is their official London residence and a working palace, containing offices for all their staff. Every day, tourists cluster around the railings of the building to watch the Changing of the Guard, in which one set of Foot Guards, from the Queen's Guard, comes off duty and is replaced by another. The proper name for this ceremony is Guard Mounting, but it is universally known by its more informal term, and it continues to be one of the most popular, traditional and evocative sights London has to offer.

THE QUEEN'S GALLERY
Buckingham Gate, SW1

If you stand little chance of securing a private invitation to Buckingham Palace (see page 16) or Windsor Castle, the Queen's Gallery is the place to visit if you want to see some of the many items that belong in the Royal Collection on display.

The gallery was created at the suggestion of Queen Elizabeth II (born 1926) and her husband, Prince Philip (born 1921), and it opened on 25 July 1962. It has interesting architectural connections, as it stands on the site of a pavilion that was built on the south-west side of Buckingham Palace in 1831. This was designed by John Nash as an Ionic temple, but was converted into a private chapel for Queen Victoria in 1843. During the Second World War, the chapel was completely destroyed in a German bombing raid on 13 September 1940, much to the regret of George VI (1936–52).

In the late 1990s, it was decided that the Queen's Gallery needed to be redeveloped. John Simpson carried out the work, at a cost of over £20 million, which was provided by the Royal Collection Trust, and the gallery re-opened on 21 May 2002. Interestingly, there is still a private chapel within the Queen's Gallery, which is not open to the public.

THE ROYAL MEWS
Buckingham Palace Road, SW1

The word 'mews' comes from the distinctive noise that was made by the falcons and hawks in the royal stables in what is now Trafalgar Square (see page 62). The mews moved from its original site to its present position in 1760. George III had bought what is now Buckingham Palace (see page 16), and it made sense to locate his carriages and horses nearby. He added an indoor riding school in 1764 and renamed the stables the Royal Mews, Pimlico.

When George IV inherited both the crown and Buckingham Palace in 1820, he was gripped by his habitual complaint of building fever. He commissioned John Nash to work not only on the palace, but also the stables, which were drastically re-modelled and expanded. The mews needed further improvements during the reign of Queen Victoria to cope with its increased workload, as she was the first monarch to use the palace as her official residence and her private home. So many servants were employed by the mews that, in 1855, Victoria set up the Buckingham Palace Royal Mews School, at her own expense, for the children of her employees. This was followed by the construction of new accommodation for the families in 1859.

The Royal Mews continues to adapt to its changing needs and is still a very busy and important part of the Royal Household. It supplies all the road transport for the Queen and other members of the Royal Family. It is from here that each newly appointed foreign ambassador is conveyed in a carriage from their official residence to Buckingham Palace to kiss the Queen's hands, returning to their quarters after the ceremony.

The Royal Mews is open to the public, who can view whichever modes of transport are not in use that day. Each of the state coaches, which are among the highlights on show, was built for a special purpose. The Gold State Coach was made

BELOW: *The Gold State Coach is only used on very special occasions – for coronations and jubilees. Its occupants here are George V and Queen Mary.*

ABOVE: *The Guards' Museum contains the uniforms and medals of its five regiments, which all belong to the Household Division.*

THE GUARDS' MUSEUM
Wellington Barracks, Birdcage Walk, SW1

As its name suggests, this museum commemorates the five Guards regiments of the British army, and is housed in their headquarters at Wellington Barracks. The five regiments are the Coldstream Guards, the Grenadier Guards, the Irish Guards, the Scots Guards and the Welsh Guards, and they all form part of the Household Division. The museum was opened in 1988 and has displays of uniforms and medals, as well as dioramas showing some of the battles in which the Guards have fought.

The Coldstream, Grenadier and Scots Guards were formed after Charles II's restoration to the throne in 1660. They comprised two regiments from the King's Body Guard and one from Oliver Cromwell's New Model Army, which was formed during the Civil War. The Irish Guards were formed during the reign of Queen Victoria and the Welsh Guards during the First World War.

BIRDCAGE WALK
SW1

Although we often take them for granted, London street names can tell us a great deal about the local history of an area. Birdcage Walk is a classic example of this, as it derives its name from James I's aviary, which once stood here. Charles II shared his grandfather's love of birds and expanded the aviary after he came to the throne in 1660. It was during this time that St James's Park (see page 21) was re-modelled and Birdcage Walk created. It

for George III in 1762, and it is only used for coronations and jubilees. Riding in it made Queen Victoria feel sick, and George VI described the trip to his coronation as 'one of the most uncomfortable rides I have ever had in my life'. Let us hope that the Irish Coach – so-called because it was made in Dublin – which Queen Victoria bought in 1852 and is used annually for the State Opening of Parliament, is more comfortable. Another carriage was added in 1910 when George V bought the Glass State Coach for use at royal weddings.

In addition to the carriages, the Royal Mews is home to the 30 or more working horses that help the Royal Family to carry out their official and ceremonial duties. These animals consist mostly of Cleveland Bays, which are the only British breed of carriage horse, and Windsor Greys, which traditionally pull the monarch's carriages. Motorized transport is also in evidence, including a fleet of Rolls Royce Phantoms, which do not carry number-plates.

forms the southern border of the park, running from Buckingham Gate to Horse Guards Road.

Although the public was allowed into St James's Park during Charles II's reign, only the hereditary Grand Falconer (the Duke of St Albans) and the Royal Family were permitted to travel along Birdcage Walk. In later years, houses were built along the road and it was opened to the public.

ST JAMES'S PARK
SW1

This is the oldest royal park in London and it has the added distinction of being surrounded by three royal palaces: Buckingham Palace (see page 16), the Palace of Westminster (see page 36) and St James's Palace (see page 25). Although it is now part of one of the most prestigious areas in London, it began life as a boggy field next to a leper hospital for women. The site of the hospital has also come up in the world, as it is now occupied by St James's Palace.

Henry VIII (1509–47), who always had such a canny eye for property, saw the potential of this area when he acquired it in 1532. He knocked down the hospital in order to build a palace, and drained the field to create a tiltyard and bowling alley, as well as a nursery for his collection of deer. Succeeding monarchs enjoyed the park and altered it to suit their needs: Elizabeth I (1558–1603) staged pageants and fêtes here, while James I improved the drainage so he could create a formal garden complete with a menagerie that included two crocodiles. Along with many royal properties, St James's Park suffered during the Interregnum (1649–60), the period between the end of the English Civil War and the Restoration, during which Charles II was in exile, and Londoners cut down many of the trees and burnt them for fuel.

Charles II rescued the park from neglect after he came to the throne. He acquired a further 36 acres (14.5 hectares) of land and had the grounds landscaped in what was then the highly fashionable, formal French style typified by the designs of André Le Nôtre (1613–1700). One of Charles's lasting legacies is the park's canal, which was formed by merging some small ponds into one long stretch of water. Charles was particularly fond of the waterway, and used to parade around it with his mistresses – he was even known to swim in it on occasion. Such activities took place in full view of the public, who were admitted into the park for the first time during Charles's reign.

By the time Queen Anne (1702–14) came to the throne, the park had lost its grandeur and been colonized by prostitutes. However, it was gradually reclaimed by polite society and, in 1814, the Prince Regent held a spectacular gala here to celebrate the 16th anniversary of the Battle of the Nile and the centenary of the House of Hanover's British rule. A Chinese pagoda was built for the occasion, but tragically it caught fire during the fireworks display, killing one man and injuring five others.

Pelican Park

Many renovations and alterations have been carried out to St James's Park since then. However, some things have not changed. The park is home to several pelicans, which were first introduced when a Russian ambassador gave a pair of the birds to Charles II.

QUEEN VICTORIA MEMORIAL AND GARDENS
SW1

When Queen Victoria died in 1901 she had been on the throne for nearly 64 years. The Queen Victoria Memorial Committee was set up in the year of her death to create some suitable monuments in her memory. One of the plans was to give The Mall (see page 32) a radical facelift and make Buckingham Palace the focal point of this long stretch of avenue. It seemed fitting to erect a massive memorial to the late queen outside the east front of the palace, and Thomas Brock was commissioned to create it.

The memorial was finally unveiled in 1911. It had taken so long to complete that Victoria's son, Edward VII, was also dead and the task of unveiling the memorial fell to her grandson, who was by now George V (1910–36). In a crowd-pleasing moment, he knighted Brock during the ceremony.

If the late queen had been able to scrutinize the monument, she would undoubtedly have been pleased. In typical Victorian style, it is heavy with allegory, including marble carvings that represent Charity, Truth and Justice. The seated figure of

OPPOSITE: *The Queen Victoria Memorial is topped by a gilded figure of Victory, which has the figures of Constancy and Courage at her feet.*

Victoria is at the centre of the memorial, gazing down the Mall.

Aston Webb (1849–1930) was commissioned to transform the area around the memorial into the Queen Victoria Memorial Gardens. The original plan was for simple grass in the gardens, but elaborate flowerbeds were created at the request of Edward VII.

GREEN PARK
SW1

When Henry VIII acquired the leper hospital of St James-the-Less, which he knocked down so he could build St James's Palace (see page 25), the adjoining graveyard came with it. Henry enclosed it, but it was not made into a royal park until Charles II laid out some pleasant walks in it. Charles also built a snow house in which cold drinks were kept in the summer; the mound that covered this snow house is still visible opposite 119 Piccadilly.

Having started life as the burial ground of a leper hospital, Green Park continued to have a rather insalubrious reputation well into the 18th century. It became a prime location for men to fight duels, and when Londoners were not dodging flying bullets they also had to cope with the unwelcome attention of highwaymen, who were particularly fond of this park.

Green Park is roughly triangular in shape, bounded to the north-west by Piccadilly, to the south by Constitution Hill (see page 16) and to the north-east by Queen's Walk. This latter walk was laid out for Queen Caroline (1683–1737), the wife of George II. A small pavilion was built here for her, in which she enjoyed sitting. She was considered to be much more intelligent than her husband, and a popular rhyme of the time ran:

'You may strut, dapper George, but 'twill all be in vain, We all know 'tis Caroline, not you, that reign.'

SPENCER HOUSE
St James's Place, SW1

Spencer House is the ancestral home of the late Diana, Princess of Wales (1961–97), and, as its name suggests, it was once owned by her family. The 1st Earl Spencer bought a lease on the site and commissioned the architect John Vardy (1718–65) to build a house for him. The work was carried out between 1756–66, with James 'Athenian' Stuart (1713–88) superseding Vardy in 1758.

The finished house was at the forefront of neo-classical design and was considered to be one of the finest homes in 18th-century London. It was important for the Spencer family that it should be as grand as possible, as they occupied an elevated social position and needed a house to reflect this. They had many links with the monarchy, and both the 4th and 6th Earls served as Lord Chamberlain of the Royal Household. In July 1981, the Spencer's most dazzling association with royalty occurred when Lady Diana Spencer married Prince Charles.

Spencer House continued as the London home of the Spencer family until 1895, when they leased it out. Today, the house has been restored to its original 18th-century splendour, complete with artefacts borrowed from the Royal Collection.

CLARENCE HOUSE
Stable Yard Road, St James's Palace, SW1

For almost 50 years, from 1953–2002, Clarence House was synonymous with one woman – Queen Elizabeth, the Queen Mother (1900–2002). It became her London home after the death of her husband, George VI, in February 1952. In fact, she swapped homes with her daughter, who succeeded to the throne as Elizabeth II and who had been living at Clarence House with her husband, Prince Philip, since 1949.

Clarence House is one of the many buildings within the precincts of St James's Palace, and was built by John Nash between 1825–27 for the Duke of Clarence, for whom it was named and who

BELOW: *This is how the Morning Room at Clarence House looked when Alfred, Duke of Edinburgh lived here in the 19th century.*

OPPOSITE: *Charles I was sentenced to death after being found guilty of treason against his people. He spent his last night at St James's Palace.*

became William IV in 1830. The interior design was deliberately kept plain because the duke, in almost comical contrast to his brother George IV, disliked anything that was ornate or gilded. Such was his loathing of elaborate decorative schemes that, even when he succeeded to the throne, he continued to live at Clarence House, as he heartily disliked the fussy interiors at Buckingham Palace. Once, when shown one of the Old Masters collected by his brother, William IV commented, 'Aye, it seems pretty – I dare say it is. My brother was fond of this sort of nick-nackery.' The cramped living quarters meant that William and his queen, Adelaide (1792–1849), had to tidy away their belongings before holding levées in their apartments.

After William IV died in 1837 and his widow, Adelaide, moved to Bushy Park (see page 120) and Marlborough House (see page 28), Clarence House became the home of a series of royal residents. Queen Victoria's mother, the Duchess of Kent, lived here from 1841–61, enabling her to keep an eye on her daughter and bask in her reflected glory. From 1866–1900, Victoria's second son, Alfred, Duke of Edinburgh (1844–1900) lived here with his wife, Marie, who was the daughter of Tsar Alexander II. A Russian Orthodox chapel was built for her on the first floor. The next inhabitants were Arthur, Duke of Connaught and Strathearn (1850–1942), and his wife Louise (1860–1917). The duke was Queen Victoria's favourite son; he lived here from 1900 until his death, after which Clarence House was given to the War Organization of the British Red Cross and Order of St John of Jerusalem for the remainder of the Second World War.

Having been turned into offices during the war, it took a long time to convert Clarence House back into a comfortable home when it was needed for the newlywed Duke and Duchess of Edinburgh in November 1947; they did not move in for a further 18 months. Their daughter, Princess Anne, was born here in August 1950. The couple moved out soon after the duchess became Elizabeth II, and Clarence House was once again overrun with decorators, who were now preparing for the arrival of the widowed

Queen Mother and her younger daughter, Princess Margaret (1930–2002). From 1970, Clarence House became the focus of attention on 4 August each year as crowds gathered in Stable Yard Road to celebrate the Queen Mother's birthday.

After her mother's death in March 2002, the Queen decided that Prince Charles and his two sons, the Princes William and Harry, should move into Clarence House. The following year, parts of the refurbished Clarence House were opened to the public for the first time.

ST JAMES'S PALACE
SW1

It is one of life's ironies that the palace from which the Court of St James – to give the British court its official title – operates was built on the site of a leper hospital. St James's Hospital was believed to date from before the Norman Conquest of 1066, although the earliest record of it comes from the 12th century. Henry VIII, who certainly had a marvellous ability to spot promising areas of land, bought the hospital in 1532, with the intention of building a palace here. The surrounding land was marshy, but it was drained and then became St James's Park (see page 21).

The palace was completed for Henry in 1540, although all that remains from his era is the gatehouse to Colour Court. His daughter, Mary I (1553–58), died in the palace, and Henry's other daughter, Elizabeth I, took refuge here during the threatened invasion by the Spanish Armada in July 1588. That August, Elizabeth left St James's Palace in the state barge and sailed to Tilbury. The following day, she addressed her troops there with a rousing speech that has become world famous: 'I know I have the body of a weak and feeble woman, but I have the heart and stomach of a king, and of a king of England too.'

Births and Deaths
In January 1649, after the English Civil War had ended, the unthinkable happened. Charles I (1625–49) was found guilty of treason against his

people and sentenced to death. He spent his last night at St James's Palace rather than at Whitehall Palace, the primary royal residence of the time, because he did not want to be kept awake by the sound of workmen assembling his scaffold. On the morning of his execution, Charles took Holy Communion in the Chapel Royal within St James's Palace and walked through St James's Park to the Banqueting House (see page 33) from where he was taken to be executed.

Whitehall Palace had survived a number of fires (a universal hazard at the time), but it did not withstand a blaze that broke out in 1698, and so St James's Palace became the official London residence of the Royal Family. It was already popular with royalty, as many royal babies had been born here, including the future Charles II in 1630 and his brother James II in 1633, as well as James's daughters, Mary II (1689–94) and Queen Anne. Both queens lived here in turn, after which the crown passed to their Hanoverian cousin, George I (1714–27), and his descendants.

The Hanoverian kings had very difficult relationships with their eldest sons, which often culminated in dramatic arguments. One such event took place in 1737, when the English court was visiting Hampton Court Palace (see page 121). George II had a blazing row with his eldest son, Frederick, Prince of Wales (1707–51), whom he despised. The argument centred on the imminent birth of Frederick's first child. George II and Caroline had little faith in their son's ability to father a healthy child, and the queen wanted to be present at the birth to make sure there was no attempt to substitute another baby for a weakling prince or princess. Caroline's orders were ignored by Frederick, who rushed his wife, Augusta of Saxe-Gotha-Altenburg (1719–72), to St James's Palace under cover of darkness the moment she went into labour. The thwarted king and queen arrived in London too late to witness the birth of their granddaughter, also called Augusta, and were so incensed that they ordered Frederick to leave the palace. He and his family went to live at Leicester House; Leicester Square now stands on the site of this royal property.

A Marriage Made in Hell

There were more dramas when George, Prince of Wales, who was born at the palace in 1762, married Caroline of Brunswick (1768–1821) in the palace's Chapel Royal in 1795. This wedding had all the elements of a farce, as the prince could not bring himself to look at his bride – he considered her extremely unprepossessing, not least because of her aversion to soap and hot water – and instead gazed at his mistress, Lady Jersey. The prince was also drunk, so much so that he had to be helped up the aisle, and at one point it looked as though he would have dearly loved to make a run for it.

Cumberland's Curious Incident

Another bizarre incident at the palace concerned the prince's younger brother, Ernest, Duke of Cumberland (1771–1851). Scandalous stories circulated about the duke, including one that claimed he had fathered a son by his sister, Princess Sophia. He was heartily disliked, as was proved on 31 March 1810, when an attempt was made on his life. At the time, the duke was living in York House, one of the residences within the precincts of St James's Palace. He was savagely attacked in the early hours by an assailant wielding a knife or a sword. The duke screamed for help and everyone came running except his Corsican valet, Joseph Sellis, who was found in his quarters with his throat cut. At first, it looked as though he was the assassin and had committed suicide immediately after the attack. However, there were some strange anomalies, which were never answered satisfactorily, but glossed over at the subsequent inquiry, which returned a verdict of suicide. Sellis was left-handed, but his neck had been cut by someone who was right-handed; his head was almost severed from his body, which is an impossibility in cases of suicide; and a blood-stained cut-throat razor was found on a nearby chest of drawers, with the suggestion that Sellis had neatly placed it there after slashing his throat, something that seems unlikely in the extreme given the extent of his injuries. Far from committing suicide, it looked as though Sellis had been murdered, but by whom? By the duke himself, by his other valet, Neale, or by someone else? Rumours abounded, but the mystery has never been solved. After the duke's brother, William IV, died in June 1837, the Duke of Cumberland became King of Hanover and styled himself Ernest I. Salic Law barred Queen Victoria from the throne of Hanover, although there were no such obstructions to the British throne.

A Home for Mrs Jordan

When William IV was still the Duke of Clarence, he was given apartments within St James's Palace, and it was here that he lived with his mistress, the comic actress Mrs Jordan, between 1790–1811. Mrs

Jordan, whose real name was Dorothea Bland, already had four illegitimate children, and she bore 10 more for the duke. They were given the surname Fitzclarence and, remarkably for an age in which infant mortality blighted virtually every family, all survived to adulthood. The relationship between William and Mrs Jordan, which was very happy, only ended because pressure was put on the duke to marry and produce an heir. However, his affection for Mrs Jordan continued, and in 1834 he asked for a statue of her, modelled by Sir Francis Chantrey, to be placed in Westminster Abbey 'beside the monument of the Queens'. The Dean of Westminster refused to grant the request. In 1975, the statue was finally given a royal setting when it was erected in Buckingham Palace.

BELOW: *The Tudor gatehouse leading to Colour Court in St James's Palace is easily identified by its diagonal clock and tall, octagonal turrets.*

A Working Palace

St James's Palace is still the official residence of the sovereign, although reigning monarchs have lived at Buckingham Palace since the accession of Queen Victoria. Nevertheless, St James's Palace remains a working palace and contains several important royal departments, including the Central Chancery of the Orders of Knighthood. It also continues to be the home of several members of the Royal Family.

THE QUEEN'S CHAPEL
Marlborough Gate, SW1

This chapel had an inauspicious start to life because it was built for a royal marriage that did not take place. In 1623, Inigo Jones (1573–1652) was commissioned to build the church for the Infanta of Spain, who was going to be the child bride of Charles I until wedding negotiations between Spain and England ran into trouble and the entire event was cancelled. The building work also ground to a halt, but it began again when Charles married Henrietta Maria (1609–69) in 1625.

When Charles II married Catherine of Braganza (1638–1705), the church was refurbished to cater for her Roman Catholicism. Her religion meant that she could not be crowned as the English queen, as she could not take part in the Anglican coronation ritual, but at least she had a place in which she could worship.

BELOW: *Marlborough House's first tenant was Sarah, Duchess of Marlborough, who was a close friend of Queen Anne until they fell out.*

A variety of different religious services has been held here for English monarchs. Dutch Reformed services were held for William III (1689–1702) and his wife Mary II; the Hanoverians attended German Lutheran services and Queen Alexandra (1844–1925) attended services in her native Danish. Today, the services are Anglican once more.

MARLBOROUGH HOUSE
Pall Mall, SW1

In the early 18th century, Queen Anne granted a 50-year lease to her great friend, Sarah, Duchess of Marlborough (1660–1744) on a parcel of land adjoining St James's Palace so she could build a house. The duchess laid the foundation stone herself in 1709 and, always impatient with architects and builders, played a large role in supervising the work. The house was completed in 1711 and the duchess lived here until she died here in 1744.

The lease returned to the Crown in 1817 and the house was prepared for the next residents, who were the Prince Regent's daughter, Princess Charlotte (1796–1817), and her husband, Prince Leopold of Saxe-Coburg-Saalfield (1790–1865). However, Charlotte died in childbirth in November, and her son was stillborn, so the prince lived here by himself until he left in 1831 to become King of the Belgians. When William IV died in 1837, his widow, Queen Adelaide, moved into the house, remaining here until her death in 1849.

Bright Young Things

If the first half of the 19th century at Marlborough House was characterized by sadness, the atmosphere changed dramatically in the early 1860s when the Prince of Wales, later Edward VII, moved in. This was the start of what became known as the 'Marlborough House Set': a group of fashionable and well-connected young people whose lives revolved around the Prince and Princess of Wales. It was all rather racy and daring, contrasting with the high moral tone of Queen Victoria's reign.

Dower House

When Victoria died in 1901 and Edward VII and Queen Alexandra moved to Buckingham Palace, their eldest son, the future George V, lived at Marlborough House as the Prince of Wales. It had special significance for him because it was his birthplace and that of most of his siblings. Queen Alexandra returned to her old home in 1910 when her husband died, and lived here until her death in 1925. Queen Mary (1867–1953) became a widow on the death of George V in 1936, and so once again another dowager queen lived at Marlborough House until her death. There are plaques in Marlborough Road in memory of both Queen Alexandra and Queen Mary.

Crisis

In the autumn of 1936, Marlborough House was the scene of much heart-searching, as the abdication crisis reached a climax. Edward VIII (1936), who had yet to be crowned after the death of his father, George V, was conducting a love affair with a divorced American woman, Mrs Wallis Simpson, much to the horror of both his family and the government. It was becoming increasingly apparent that he had to choose between the throne and his lover, and he eventually chose the latter. His brother, the Duke of York, was at Marlborough House when he heard the shattering news that Edward VIII had decided to abdicate, and that he would now have to become George VI. He wept on his mother's shoulder when he was told this.

Marlborough House was given to the government in 1959 and was used as a Commonwealth Centre. It is now the home of the Commonwealth Secretariat.

PALL MALL
SW1

We owe the name of this street to the 16th-century delight in a game called *pallo a maglio*, which, roughly translated, means 'ball to mallet'. It became popular during the reign of Charles II, who was often to be seen playing it with one or more of his many mistresses in St James's Park. The original alley for pell mell, as the game was called in Britain, was dressed with a layer of powdered cockleshells and ran just inside the wall of the park. However, the alley was almost unusable each summer because passing carriages sent up choking clouds of dust that inconvenienced the players. A new alley was built to the north of the first one, away from passing traffic. It was called Catherine Street in honour of Charles II's wife, but was popularly called Pall Mall and has kept that name ever since.

Royal Favours

All of Pall Mall, with one notable exception, belongs to the Crown. The exception is number 79,

ABOVE: *Edward VIII was adored by the general public, who were shocked when he abdicated to marry Mrs Simpson in December 1936.*

which was once the home of Nell Gwyn (1657–87), one of Charles II's most famous mistresses. Nell complained to Charles when she was granted a lease on the property and insisted on being given the freehold, rather cheekily saying that she 'had always conveyed free under the Crown and always would'. When she died in 1687 the house passed to their son, the Duke of St Albans (1670–1726), but he was forced to hand it over to his creditors six years later.

Another royal alliance took place in the same house in 1766 when George III's brother, William, Duke of Gloucester (1743–1805), secretly married the Dowager Countess of Waldegrave; unfortunately they managed to make each other very miserable. Interestingly, George's youngest brother, Henry, Duke of Cumberland (1745–90), also chose 79 Pall Mall in which to marry secretly in 1770. His bride was Mrs Anne Houghton, a widow, but this marriage was a success. Happy or not, both marriages were a threat to the royal succession, and

Parliament passed the Royal Marriages Act in 1772, ruling that any royal marriage that took place without the consent of the sovereign was automatically rendered illegal.

The existence of the Royal Marriages Act – which is still in place today – did not deter George III's son, the Prince of Wales, who also married in secret. His bride, Mrs Fitzherbert, lived at number 105 between 1789–96, when her relationship with the prince was going through a low point. Their marriage was never valid in law, which was just as well as the prince later married Princess Caroline of Brunswick without first ridding himself of Mrs Fitzherbert.

Pall Mall Princesses

Some official members of the Royal Family have also lived in Pall Mall. Princess Helena (1846–1923), a daughter of Queen Victoria, lived at numbers 77–78 from 1902–23, and her daughters, Princess Helena Victoria and Princess Marie Louise, remained in their family home until 1947. Princess Helena died at Schomberg House, numbers 80–82, in 1923; it has retained its original façade although the rest of the house was reconstructed in the late 1950s. Sadly, Nell Gwyn's house was demolished in the 1860s and replaced by the present building.

ST JAMES'S SQUARE
SW1

It is 21 June 1815 – the height of the Napoleonic Wars. Mrs Edward Boehm, a society hostess, is giving a glittering ball at her house, 16 St James's Square. The Prince Regent is her honoured guest and everything is going splendidly until there is a commotion at the front door. A bloodstained, grubby man, his army uniform in tatters, rushes up the staircase and grabs the prince. Mrs Boehm is anxious – who is this impostor? He reveals himself to be Major the Honourable Henry Percy, bearing the astonishing news of England's victory at the Battle of Waterloo three days before. To prove his story, he lays the eagles of the French army at the prince's feet. Consternation! Delighted, the prince makes Percy a colonel right there and then, but Mrs Boehm is furious because her party is ruined, forgotten in the succeeding jubilation.

This is not the only royal event to have taken place in St James's Square, which is one of the most prestigious addresses in Westminster. Today, it is home to businesses and various institutions, but in the past the buildings were the private homes of many important people. The original Norfolk House, at number 3, was the birthplace of George III in 1738. His daughter-in-law, Queen Caroline, stayed at number 17 in 1820, during the investigations into her alleged adultery. The hearing took place at the House of Lords, to which she travelled in a state carriage. Cheering crowds collected around her house each morning and evening, calling for her to appear at the windows, and she was always delighted to grant their wishes.

Number 21 was once the home of two other notorious women connected with royalty: Arabella Churchill and Catherine Sedley, who were both mistresses of the Duke of York, later James II. His brother, Charles II, had such a low opinion of the women that he once said they must have been inflicted on the duke by his priests as a penance.

There is a bronze statue in the garden at the centre of the square, depicting William III as a Roman general on horseback. A molehill lies under

the horse's hooves, as a reminder of the animal that tripped up William's horse in 1702 and caused his death from the subsequent fall.

WATERLOO PLACE
SW1

Waterloo Place was built to link the southern end of Regent Street with what was then Carlton House, the Prince Regent's private residence. It was begun in 1816 and named in honour of Britain's triumph at the Battle of Waterloo.

Although Carlton House was pulled down in 1826 and Carlton House Terrace built on the land, Waterloo Place continues to have strong royal associations. A bronze equestrian statue of Edward VII, built by Sir Bertram Mackennal and erected in 1922, stands to the south of Pall Mall. It is an appropriate position for this king as he enjoyed belonging to the many gentlemen's clubs of St James's and Pall Mall, and patronized them most assiduously.

ABOVE: *An equestrian statue of William III stands in the centre of St James's Square, which has witnessed many memorable royal events.*

The Grand Old Duke of York

Nevertheless, the most imposing feature of Waterloo Place is the Duke of York Column, which stands above the Duke of York Steps that lead down to the Mall (see page 32). There have been many Dukes of York over the centuries but the one celebrated here is Frederick (1763–1827), who was the second son of George III and the brother of George IV. The memorial was erected in the 1830s and consists of a very tall column designed by Benjamin Wyatt, topped by a square balcony, drum and dome on which stands a bronze statue of the duke by Sir Richard Westmacott. The joke at the time was that the statue had been placed so high in order to keep the duke away from his creditors – he had debts of about £2 million at the time of his death. The money to build the column was mostly raised by stopping one day's pay from every soldier in the army, which doubtless diminished what had been until then the duke's popularity with his men.

THE MALL
WC1

The Mall always comes into its own during royal celebrations, when it is thronged with the thousands of people who cannot get any closer to Buckingham Palace (see page 16). During the celebrations for Elizabeth II's Golden Jubilee in June 2002, the Mall was the scene of a lengthy carnival procession presided over by the Royal Family and television cameras from around the world.

As with so many other streets around this area, the Mall was created during the improvements to St James's Park (see page 21) that followed the Restoration of Charles II in 1660. The street replaced Pall Mall (see page 29) as the venue for the then popular game of pell mell, and became a busy avenue along which fashionable society strolled.

The Mall was transformed in 1903–04, as part of the national memorial to Queen Victoria who had died in 1901, although it was not completed until 1911. The original Mall was renamed Horse Ride, and its name was transferred to the new royal processional route leading from Buckingham Palace to Admiralty Arch.

A network of underground tunnels runs beneath the Mall, connecting Buckingham Palace with many major government departments and buildings, including 10 Downing Street.

HORSE GUARDS PARADE
Whitehall, SW1

This is one of the few reminders of the long-vanished Whitehall Palace, which once sprawled over this area of London. The parade ground stands on the site of the tiltyard of the Tudor palace. It was a favourite place of Henry VIII, an accomplished rider who enjoyed jousts before his increasing girth and ill-health forced him to adopt a more sedentary way of life.

Each year, Horse Guards Parade is the scene of one of the great royal ceremonies, the Trooping of the Colour. This dates back to the 18th century, and it has also been part of the official birthday celebrations of the sovereign since 1748. Tradition dictates that this official birthday always falls in the summer months, as there is then a better chance of the public ceremonials taking place on a sunny day.

The Trooping of the Colour commemorates the ancient military practice of parading (or trooping) the flags (or colours) of a battalion in front of its soldiers so they could easily recognize them on the battlefield. Each year, one of the five regiments of the Foot Guards (Coldstream, Grenadier, Irish, Scots and Welsh) takes it in turn to be the chosen battalion whose colours are trooped to the musical accompaniment of the massed regimental bands. In addition, the sovereign inspects the Foot Guards and the Household Cavalry and takes the salute. Elizabeth II used to do this on horseback, riding side-saddle in the uniform of whichever Guards regiment was trooping, but since 1987 she has attended the ceremony in her own clothes and in her own carriage.

The Horse Guards building is guarded daily by four members of the Household Cavalry: two on horseback and two on foot. Those on horseback are relieved every hour, but the others have to stand motionless for two hours at a stretch. The Changing of the Guard also takes place here daily, during which the Old Guard is relieved by the New Guard.

BELOW: *The Trooping of the Colour only takes place once a year in Horse Guards Parade, but the Horse Guards can be seen here every day.*

The building itself was designed by William Kent (1684–1748) and completed by John Vardy in the 1750s. The clock in the tower has a black dot over the two, to commemorate the time of Charles I's execution on the other side of the road, outside the Banqueting House (see below) on 30 January 1649.

THE BANQUETING HOUSE
Whitehall, SW1

Just before 2 o'clock on the afternoon of 30 January 1649, Charles I stepped out of one of the first-floor windows of the Banqueting House on to a specially made scaffold to face his executioner. Throngs of people on the street below jostled one another for a better view of what was to come: the beheading of the reigning monarch for treason. His crime was to have allowed the Stuart belief in the Divine Right of Kings to clash with the increasing power of Parliament, triggering the English Civil War; he was therefore charged with making war on his subjects.

To Kill a King
It was a chilly day and Charles had taken the precaution of wearing two shirts, in case any shivers from the cold might be mistaken for fear.

ABOVE: *The Banqueting House is all that remains of Whitehall Palace, which burnt down in 1698. Its ceiling is decorated with nine Rubens panels.*

He was dignified to the last, saying to Dr Juxon, the Bishop of London, who was attending him: 'I go from a corruptible to an incorruptible Crown, where no disturbance can be. Remember.' He could not address the people directly, as he was kept so far away from them – Parliament wanted to prevent him making a speech. As the watching crowd saw the axe fall, an onlooker recorded: 'There was such a dismal universal groan amongst the thousands of people who were in sight of it, as it were with one consent, as I never heard before and desire I may not hear again.'

The choice of the Banqueting House as the place of execution was no accident: it was part of Whitehall Palace, which had been a royal residence since Henry VIII's reign, and the ceiling of the main room was decorated with Rubens paintings that celebrated the Stuart dynasty. The entire event was a conclusive statement of the Parliamentarian repudiation of monarchy and all it stood for.

The daring experiment of a republican Britain lasted until 1660, when Charles II was restored to the throne (having succeeded to it in theory

WESTMINSTER ABBEY
SW1

ABOVE: *The 10 niches on the West Front of Westminster Abbey contain statues of modern Christian martyrs, and were unveiled in 1998.*

on the day of his father's death). Once again, the Banqueting House was the focus because the formal restoration ceremony took place here on 29 May 1660.

'A Foul Protestant Wind'

A third major event in British history took place here on 13 February 1689, when the crown was offered to the Prince and Princess of Orange, who accepted it to become William III and Mary II. They took over the crown from Mary's father, James II, whose pro-Catholic stance made him too unpopular to remain king. The weathervane on top of the Banqueting House is said to have been placed here by James so he could watch for the 'foul Protestant wind' that would bring William and Mary to Britain. It duly blew them to Devon in November 1688, at which point James felt it was prudent to hot-foot it to France.

Although the rest of Whitehall Palace was destroyed in a fire in 1698, the Banqueting House was left unscathed. It was turned into a Chapel Royal, then later a museum, but is now once again a venue for important public occasions. President George W. Bush made a speech here in November 2003.

As a seemingly endless succession of buses and taxis hurtle around Parliament Square, their exhaust fumes addin`g further accretions of dirt to those that have already collected on the English Gothic stone façade of Westminster Abbey, it takes a monumental effort to imagine how the building might have looked in a less hectic age.

In the 11th century, this was a marshy stretch of land outside the city walls, on which Edward the Confessor (1042–66) built a cruciform church to accompany his new palace. The church was consecrated on 28 December 1065 and Edward died early in January 1066. He was buried before the high altar. On Christmas Day that same year, William the Conqueror was crowned here, setting the precedent that all future coronations should take place in Westminster Abbey. There have only been three exceptions to this: Edward V (1483), who was murdered before he could be crowned; Lady Jane Grey (1553), who only reigned for nine days before being deposed and sent to the Tower of London and subsequently executed (see page 55); and Edward VIII, who abdicated in 1936 before his coronation.

A massive construction project began in 1245, when Henry III (1216–72) began to rebuild the abbey. He had added a Lady Chapel in 1220, but now he wanted to create a building that was suitable for the coronations and burials of sovereigns, and he looked to European cathedrals for inspiration. This is when the abbey that we see today first began to take shape, with the central crossing between the Quire and the Sanctuary Steps large enough to be the focus of coronations. Henry also created a special shrine to St Edward the Confessor, who had been canonized in 1161 and is the only British king to have ever received such an honour.

Many monarchs have added to the history of the abbey in their own way. In March 1413, Henry IV (1399–1413) was making plans to visit the Holy Land and was praying before St Edward's Shrine when he was taken ill. He was carried into the Jerusalem Chamber, which was then part of the medieval lodgings of the abbey's abbot, at which point he regained consciousness and asked where he was. When told that he was in Jerusalem, he realized he was going to die: it had long been prophesied that he would die in Jerusalem.

One of the most bizarre events in the abbey's history took place on 19 July 1821, when George IV came here to be crowned. His flamboyant and dramatic coronation garments, which he had designed himself, were astonishing enough, to say nothing of the make-up that was caked on his face and which melted in the summer heat, but these paled into insignificance as events unfolded. George's marriage to Caroline of Brunswick had long been over in all but name. Nevertheless, Caroline fully expected to be crowned queen at the same time as her estranged husband was made king. Crowds lining the streets cheered as her carriage drove from her house in South Audley Street to the abbey, but when she arrived every door she tried to enter was shut in her face. She finally managed to get through a door at Poet's Corner but was told that there was no place for her in the abbey and she would have to leave. Reluctantly, she did so. On her way back to South Audley Street the crowd turned against her, with boos and cat-calls. Three weeks later, she was dead.

A Modern Coronation
On 2 June 1953, history was made when the coronation of Elizabeth II at Westminster Abbey was televised. This was the first time that television cameras had been allowed to record such a sacred service, and virtually none of the Queen's advisers was in favour of it. However, she ignored their protests and, as a result, many of her subjects bought their first television sets expressly so they could watch the crowning of their new queen. The Coronation Chair on which Elizabeth II sat is on view in the abbey. It was created for Edward I (1272–1307) in 1296, after he stole the Stone

of Scone on which many Scots kings had been crowned, and triumphantly brought it back to England. The chair was first used at the coronation of Edward II (1307–27) in 1308 and has been an integral part of every coronation since then. Today, the Stone of Scone is back in Scotland, having been returned to Edinburgh Castle in 1996.

BELOW: *Every coronation of an English monarch has taken place at Westminster Abbey since William the Conqueror was crowned here in 1066.*

Royal Resting Place

In common with St George's Chapel, Windsor, Westminster Abbey is the burial place of many kings and queens, and several of them lie in the Henry VII chapel. The bodies of Henry VII (1485–1509) himself and his queen, Elizabeth of York (1466–1503), are behind the altar. Enemies in life are near neighbours in death: Elizabeth I lies next to her half-sister, Mary I, and close by is the marble tomb of her cousin, Mary, Queen of Scots, whose death Elizabeth ordered. The abbey also contains the remains of Edward I (1272–1307), Richard II (1377–99), Henry V (1413–22), Anne of Cleves (1515–57), James I and his consort Anne of Denmark (1574–1619) Charles II, William III and his wife Mary II, Queen Anne and her consort George of Denmark, and George II and his consort Caroline. There is also a burial urn containing what are believed to be the bones of the murdered Princes in the Tower, Edward V and his brother, Richard, Duke of York, who both vanished in 1483, thereby conveniently allowing their uncle, Richard III (1483–85), to seize the throne.

Westminster Abbey continues to be one of the focal points of national life and many important events have taken place here in recent years. There have been royal weddings, including those of Princess Elizabeth and Prince Philip in 1947, Princess Margaret and Antony Armstrong-Jones in 1960, Princess Anne and Captain Mark Phillips in 1973, and Prince Andrew and Sarah Ferguson in 1986. On 6 September 1997, the funeral of Diana, Princess of Wales took place in the abbey, followed by that of Queen Elizabeth the Queen Mother on 9 April 2002 and a memorial service for Princess Margaret on 19 April that same year. In a happier vein, the abbey was the venue for a service to celebrate the Queen's Golden Jubilee on 2 June 2003, 50 years to the day since she was crowned here and the world watched in awe.

THE PALACE OF WESTMINSTER
SW1

Today, 'the Palace of Westminster' is another name for the Houses of Parliament, but despite this it is still a royal palace and has been ever since the reign of Edward the Confessor in the 11th century. The original fortified building created by Edward was taken over by William the Conqueror (1066–87) in 1066, and in due course by his son, William Rufus (1087–1100), who built Westminster Hall in 1099. William Rufus had big plans for the hall but these were curtailed by his death – and possible murder on the orders of his brother, Henry (1100–35), who then became king. Subsequent kings improved the hall, and it now has the widest unsupported hammerbeam roof in the country. Westminster Hall is still in use as a vestibule for the House of Commons, but it comes into its own for important state occasions. For instance, the lying-in-state of Edward VII in 1910, and that of Queen Elizabeth the Queen Mother in 2002, both took place here.

From the 13th century until 1882, Westminster Hall was the home of the Law Courts and therefore was witness to some notable trials. In 1536, when Henry VIII had to find a way of

BELOW: *Big Ben rises above the Palace of Westminster. The great bell first tolled for the funeral of a monarch in 1910, for Edward VII.*

ridding himself of his second wife, Anne Boleyn (*c.* 1507–36), she was accused of adultery with five men (including her brother, Lord Rochford) and of conspiring to kill the king. These were undoubtedly trumped-up charges and the outcome of the trial was a foregone conclusion. Anne and her brother were tried at the great hall in the Tower of London (see page 55). The other four men were tried at Westminster Hall, found guilty and sentenced to death. Anne and her brother were also found guilty and received the same sentence, which was swiftly carried out.

Remember, Remember

In 1606, Guy Fawkes was tried in Westminster Hall after a failed attempt to blow up James I and Parliament; Fawkes was executed just around the corner in Old Palace Yard. However, the legacy of his actions lives on; each year the Yeomen of the Guard search the cellars, where the gunpowder was found, before the State Opening of Parliament. In 1649, in one of the most sensational trials in British history, Charles I was tried in the hall and found guilty of treason against his people and duly sentenced to death. At his trial he refused to remove his hat because he did not recognize the legitimacy of the court. The law courts moved out of Westminster Hall in 1882, but between the 1660s and this date they had shared the space with stallholders selling such wares as books, toys and clothes. It is strange to think of important trials being conducted while commerce raged all around.

Gothic redevelopment

Over the centuries, many parts of the original medieval palace were destroyed by fire. Following a blaze in 1512, Henry VIII moved out of the Palace of Westminster into Whitehall Palace. He was the last sovereign to live at Westminster and the royal apartments were taken over by parliamentary officials. Nevertheless, the building continued to be called a royal palace. In October 1834, fire swept through the medieval palace again, but this time it was virtually destroyed; only the crypt of St Stephen's Chapel, the Jewel Tower (see right) and Westminster Hall survived. It was a catastrophe, but it was also an opportunity for some imaginative redevelopment. Charles Barry (1795–1860) and Augustus Pugin (1762–1832) were commissioned as the architects for the new building, creating the Gothic structure that we know today.

ABOVE: *The Jewel Tower is one of the few areas of the original Palace of Westminster that was left standing after the catastrophic fire of 1834.*

THE JEWEL TOWER
Abingdon Street, SW1

After the disastrous fire of 1834, very little of the original Palace of Westminster (see page 36) was left standing. Happily, however, the Jewel Tower is one of the buildings that survived. It was built by Henry Yevele in 1365–66 for Edward III (1327–77) and, as its name suggests, was probably intended as a safe repository of his jewels, clothes and personal belongings. The defensive moat, which is still visible outside the tower, certainly suggests this, and succeeding monarchs used the tower for their wardrobe and jewels, although there is also a theory that the Jewel Tower was originally built as a monastic prison.

The Jewel Tower continued to be the home of the royal wardrobe until the reign of Henry VII. Parliamentary records were held here from 1621–1864, after which it was used by the Weights and Measures Office until 1938. It is now owned by English Heritage and is open to the public.

ST JOHN'S SMITH SQUARE
SW1

This building is now celebrated for the concerts that are held here, but it was once the church of St John the Evangelist and renowned for its Baroque architecture. The church was designed and built between 1714–28 by Thomas Archer (1668–1743), who was a tremendous fan of Italian architecture. St John's had the distinction of being the most expensive of the 'Fifty New Churches' that were planned for London in 1711, and was built at a cost of over £40,000.

It is popularly known as 'Queen Anne's footstool' because, so the story goes, the queen was so irritated at being asked yet again to give her approval of a church design that she kicked over the nearest footstool and said 'build it like that'. As a result, St John's was given four lofty towers that attracted a great deal of criticism. In his novel *Our Mutual Friend* (1865), Charles Dickens described the building as 'some petrified monster, frightful and gigantic, on its back with its legs in the air'.

St John's has had an eventful history, as it was badly damaged by fire in 1742 and bombed during the Second World War, after which it was rebuilt as a concert hall.

BELOW: *The four towers of St John's Smith Square attracted a great deal of criticism and abuse after the church was completed in 1728.*

BUST OF CHARLES I
St Margaret's Church, Westminster, SW1

It seems to be adding insult to injury to place a commemorative bust of Charles I in such close proximity to a statue of his old adversary, Oliver Cromwell (1599–1658), but that is what has happened at Westminster. The statue of Cromwell stands outside Westminster Hall, where Charles was tried and condemned for treason in January 1649, before being executed a few days later. Cromwell was installed as Lord Protector in Westminster Hall in 1653.

The lead bust of Charles I was placed above the east door of St Margaret's Church in 1950. It is one of three that were found in a builder's yard in Fulham that same year by Hedley Hope-Nicholson, who at the time was the secretary of the Society of King Charles the Martyr. Another of the busts sits in a niche above the main door of the Banqueting House, while the third is in private hands.

St Margaret's Church has been the parish church of the House of Commons since 1614, and is where Members of Parliament are allowed to

marry and be buried. Charles I clashed with Parliament in the 1630s over who had the most power, but he lost the argument and his head with it. However, after the Restoration in 1660, the bodies of several Parliamentarians, including John Pym, which had already been buried were exhumed and ignominiously reburied in a pit in the churchyard here.

CARLTON HOUSE TERRACE
SW1

This beautiful terrace of late Georgian houses was built between 1827–32 by John Nash, George IV's favourite architect. Nash was very familiar with this area of London as he had previously worked on Carlton House, the royal palace that was pulled down to make way for the terrace.

Carlton House first came into royal hands in 1732 when Frederick, Prince of Wales, bought it. After he died it passed to his widow, Augusta, who was the mother of George III. In due course, George gave it to his eldest son, the Prince of Wales

(later George IV), who set about turning it into one of the architectural extravaganzas for which he is still renowned.

The Prince of Wales lavished what even he described as an 'enormous' amount of money on the house. His daughter, Princess Charlotte, was born here on 7 January 1796 and her marriage to the man who later became Leopold I, King of the Belgians, also took place here on 2 May 1816.

When the prince succeeded to the throne in 1820 he knew that Carlton House was not big enough for his needs. It was pulled down, the land sold to pay for the cost of renovating Buckingham Palace, and various architectural features were used in other buildings; several of the doors went to Buckingham Palace. Carlton House Terrace was built on the site of the old house and its garden. Although little remains of the Prince Regent's ornate palace, it is still easy to imagine its grandeur and to appreciate its dominant position in such a fashionable part of London.

Chapter 2

THE CITY

Some of the greatest architectural and historic royal treasures of London, such as St Paul's Cathedral and the Guildhall, belong to its ancient City. The Tower of London is one of the most famous buildings in the world and it is still an impressive sight almost 1,000 years after it was first built. It feels as though it is part of the City of London, yet it stands outside the walls of what has long been known as 'the square mile'. London Bridge is equally famous, although the original bridge, complete with houses, has long gone.

LEFT: *The top of the Monument is adorned with a flaming urn of fire, made from copper.*

OPPOSITE: *The Tower of London has been a royal prison and place of execution, as well as the home of a royal menagerie and the Royal Mint.*

ST BARTHOLOMEW'S HOSPITAL
West Smithfield, EC1

Perhaps better known by its nickname, Barts, this is the oldest hospital in London. The institution was founded in 1123 by an Augustinian monk named Rahere, who had formerly held the position of court jester to Henry I. Rahere caught malaria while on a pilgrimage to Rome, and vowed to build a hospital for the poor in London if he survived the illness, which he did. He found a suitable site in Smithfield and called the hospital after St Bartholomew, who had appeared to him in a vision while he was sick.

Initially, the hospital was run by members of the priory of St Bartholomew, but it gradually became independent. This was just as well, as the priory was closed by Henry VIII in 1539, during the Dissolution of the Monasteries, although the hospital was allowed to continue. Nevertheless, its situation was very uncertain. In 1546, Henry VIII granted the hospital to the City of London, which permitted Barts to continue to tend London's poor. Henry also granted the hospital money and

property. The first physician, Dr Roderigo Lopez, was appointed in 1562, but he was later hanged at Tyburn, having been found guilty of trying to poison Elizabeth I.

All that is left of the medieval complex of buildings is the tower of St Bartholomew-the-Less, which is the hospital's parish church. The rest of the church was rebuilt in 1789 by George Dance the Younger (1741–1825). However, this building rotted and was rebuilt again in 1825. The hospital itself was rebuilt by James Gibbs (1682–1754), the architect of St Martin-in-the-Fields (see page 65), from 1730–59. The gateway, over which presides a statue of Henry VIII by Francis Bird (1667–1731), was built in 1702.

Barts continued to be run under the charter granted by Henry VIII until 1948, when it became part of the new National Health Service. That charter is now on display in the hospital museum, which is situated in its north wing.

THE CHURCH OF ST BARTHOLOMEW-THE-GREAT
West Smithfield, EC1

This is London's oldest parish church and was founded by Rahere in 1123. At that time, the church was part of the priory and hospital of St Bartholomew (see above), and Rahere was its first prior.

Bartholomew Fair
In 1133, Henry I gave permission for Rahere to hold a fair at the site. From that point onward, a cloth fair was held each summer around St Bartholomew's Day (24 August). Over the years this became a rowdy event, but it made money for the hospital, and continued until the 19th century.

Trouble arrived in 1539, when Henry VIII dissolved the priory in the course of his English Reformation. The nave was demolished and only the choir was left standing for the parishioners to use. The fortunes of the church then followed the religious persuasion of the reigning monarch: in 1556, some Dominican monks were allowed to return by Mary I, who was a Roman Catholic, before being expelled in 1559 by the Protestant Elizabeth I.

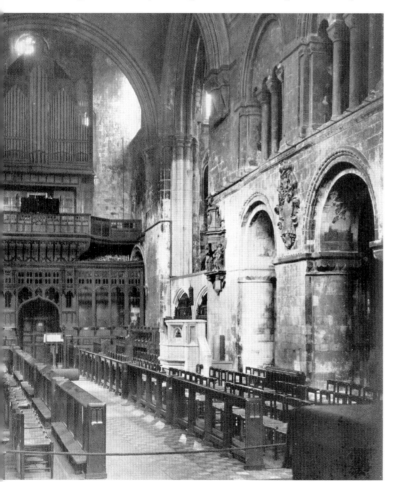

LEFT: *The church of St Bartholomew-the-Great was badly damaged during Henry VIII's Dissolution of the Monasteries in the 1530s.*

The church is still in use today, having enjoyed some unaccustomed celebrity in the 1990s after it appeared in the hit film *Four Weddings and a Funeral* (1994).

SMITHFIELD
EC1

Since 1855, Smithfield has been famous as London's largest meat market. Its current name is a corruption of 'Smooth Field', as the area was known in the Middle Ages when it played host to a horse fair every Friday. Long before then, it was a marshy swamp outside the city walls, which the Romans used as a general dumping ground.

Rebels and Religious Persecution

For centuries, Smithfield was a large open space near the city, and was therefore perfect for jousting. In 1357, it was the venue for a spectacular tournament attended by the English and French monarchs. In 1381, Smithfield was the scene of a much more serious event when the 14-year-old king, Richard II, met Wat Tyler and the poll-tax rebels. Tyler was deemed to have shown such scant respect for his monarch that he was pulled off his horse by the Lord Mayor, William Walworth, before being stabbed by another of the king's party, taken to St Bartholomew's Hospital (see page 42) for treatment, and then executed outside it.

Until the gallows were moved to Tyburn in the 1400s, Smithfield was a popular place for public executions. The Scottish rebel, William Wallace (*c.* 1272–1305), who was such a thorn in the side of Edward I, endured a hideous death here, enjoying the dubious privilege of being the first person to be hanged, drawn and quartered.

ABOVE: *Wat Tyler was executed after showing a lack of respect to Richard II in 1381.*

Smithfield was particularly busy during the religious persecutions of the Tudor monarchs. Mary I ordered more than 40 executions here, in which Protestant martyrs were burned at the stake. However, Mary's half-sister, Elizabeth I, preferred to dispatch Catholic martyrs at Tyburn. In the 1840s, archaeological excavations around the entrance of St Bartholomew-the-Great (see page 42) revealed burnt stones and charred bones – powerful evidence of these 16th-century Marian burnings.

IRELAND YARD
EC4

A fragment of wall in Ireland Yard is the only remaining trace of Blackfriars Monastery, which stood on the site between 1221–1538. The monastery was run by a community of Dominican monks who, as the name suggests, wore black habits. Their first monastery was in Shoe Lane, but they moved to the area around Ireland Yard in 1278. The monks grew rich under the patronage of Edward I, and became so influential that Parliament met here in 1311.

Henry Divorces

In 1529, a court at Blackfriars heard the divorce proceedings between Henry VIII and Katherine of Aragon (1485–1536). Henry wanted to divorce his wife because she had failed to provide him with a male heir. He claimed that the marriage was void on the grounds of consanguinity, as she had been briefly married to his late brother, Prince Arthur. Henry's marital problems led to the end of Blackfriars Monastery, as he broke with the Church of Rome when the Pope refused to recognize his divorce. In the late 1530s, Henry dissolved England's monasteries, robbing them of their considerable influence and financial assets. The church plate from Blackfriars was among the treasures he seized. The buildings themselves were given to Sir Thomas Cawarden, Keeper of the Royal Tents and Master of the Revels, although they were demolished soon after. When Mary I came to the throne, she allowed Cawarden to construct a new church for the parishioners, St Ann Blackfriars, which was destroyed during the Great Fire of London in 1666.

An arcade from the monastery was discovered in 1890 and taken to Selsdon Park, Surrey, where it was erected. In 1925, part of the choir was unearthed and taken to St Dominic's Priory on

Haverstock Hill, Hampstead. Nevertheless, the monastery is still remembered in the many place names nearby, including Friar Street, and also by the abutments, which resemble pulpits, that run along nearby Blackfriars Bridge.

ST PAUL'S CATHEDRAL
EC4

St Paul's Cathedral and Westminster Abbey are the two great centres of Anglican worship in London. The two buildings have given their respective names to the phrase 'robbing Peter to pay Paul', as the abbey is named for St Peter, and its funds were sometimes used to subsidize the cathedral of St Paul.

St Paul's dominates the summit of Ludgate Hill. A church dedicated to the saint has stood on the site since 604, when St Ethelbert, King of Kent and the first English king to embrace Christianity, founded a place of worship here. A stone church was built on the site in 685, the original church having been destroyed about 10 years previously. The Vikings ruined this building in 962, and yet another church was built, only to be

ABOVE: *After Old St Paul's was destroyed in the Great Fire of London in 1666, Charles II was involved in the design of its replacement.*

destroyed by fire in 1087. This Saxon church was replaced with a Norman cathedral, which had a generous benefactor in William II. It was made of Caen stone and became one of the largest buildings in England at the time.

As one of the most important places of worship in England, St Paul's was no stranger to royalty. In 1415, Henry V prayed here before he departed for France and his triumph at the Battle of Agincourt. He returned here after his victory and took part in a service of thanksgiving. In November 1501, Prince Arthur (1486–1502), the eldest son of Henry VII, married Katherine of Aragon in the cathedral. Arthur died five months later and, in 1509, Katherine married his younger brother, Henry VIII.

It was this marriage that led to the English Reformation, when Henry VIII created the Church of England in defiance of the Pope's refusal to grant him a divorce from Katherine so he could marry Anne Boleyn. Every church and cathedral in England suffered as a result, as Henry stripped them of their valuables, and St Paul's was no exception. In 1549, the altar was removed and replaced by an ordinary table, and the nave became a popular short cut, known as Paul's Walk, between Carter Lane and Paternoster Row. The tombs and font were used as shop counters, horses and mules clip-clopped their way along Paul's Walk, and lawyers met their clients here.

Such secular events ceased when Mary I became queen in 1553, and she reintroduced Catholic services at St Paul's. However, this second flowering of the Roman Catholic church ended in 1558 when Mary died and her Protestant half-sister, Elizabeth, succeeded to the throne. She enjoyed worshipping at St Paul's, although she was perfectly prepared to interrupt the dean's sermon when she felt it necessary. Elizabeth donated £6,000 towards the repair of the cathedral roof after it was damaged in a disastrous fire in 1561, but this was a drop in the ocean compared to the amount of money that was actually needed.

A New Beginning
The cathedral's situation worsened during the English Civil War, when Parliamentarian troops used the nave as a barracks and the building

OPPOSITE: *St Paul's Cathedral has been the venue for several royal services of thanksgiving, but coronations are always held in Westminster Abbey.*

became the haunt of shop-owners and traders once again. By the time Charles II was restored to the throne in 1660, St Paul's was a virtual ruin. Sir Christopher Wren (1632–1723) was consulted and he recommended that St Paul's should be demolished and rebuilt. This was not a popular suggestion and he was told to repair the existing cathedral instead. However, matters were taken out of everyone's hands when the Great Fire swept through the City in 1666, destroying the cathedral in the process. Wren therefore had his wish and was able to rebuild the cathedral. He received the royal warrant giving him permission to start work in 1675, and completed the new building in 1710. The slow progress of the work infuriated the authorities, who used it as an excuse to pay Wren only half his annual salary. He was not reimbursed until he petitioned Queen Anne, who was by then on the throne, for the arrears.

A statue to Queen Anne stands outside the west front of the cathedral, although it is a copy by Richard Belt, dating from 1886. The original was fashioned by the sculptor Francis Bird (1667–1731) and erected in 1712 to commemorate the completion of the cathedral. It deteriorated so

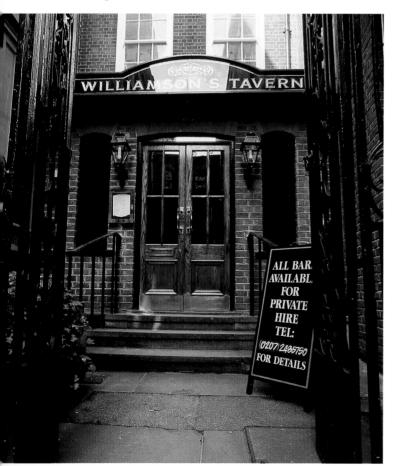

badly over the years, doubtless harmed by the noxious London air, that it had to be removed.

A Hero Rests

Unlike Westminster Abbey, which is crammed with memorials, tombs and monuments, St Paul's is relatively free of such things. However, the tomb of Admiral Lord Nelson (1758–1805) lies in the crypt. It is a black sarcophagus that was originally intended for Cardinal Wolsey (c. 1472–1530), who was Henry VIII's chief minister. Henry took a liking to the casket himself, and later considered that it might be suitable for him and his third wife, Jane Seymour (c. 1507–37). However, in the end it gathered dust in Windsor Castle for nearly three centuries before it was used for Lord Nelson's burial in January 1806.

State Ceremonies

Tradition dictates that the great royal ceremonies, such as coronations and funerals, take place in Westminster Abbey, but several state occasions have been held in St Paul's Cathedral. For instance, there was a thanksgiving service, over which Queen Anne presided, for the British victory at the Battle of Blenheim in 1704 and another thanksgiving service at the end of the Napoleonic Wars in 1814, which was attended by the Prince Regent. In 1872, there was a service of thanksgiving for the safe recovery of Edward, Prince of Wales (later Edward VII) who had nearly died from typhoid the previous year. This service was remarkable because Queen Victoria emerged from her deep mourning, following the death of Prince Albert in 1861 (also from typhoid), in order to attend it, and in doing so managed to quash the republican sentiment that was sweeping the country at the time. She retained her throne, and celebrated her Diamond Jubilee in 1897 with another service of thanksgiving at the cathedral. The sermon was given on the steps of St Paul's, while the queen listened from her open carriage. In 1901, a memorial service for Victoria was held at the cathedral at the same time as her burial service in Windsor.

LEFT: *The wrought-iron gates at the end of the alley leading to Williamson's Tavern were given to the Lord Mayor by William III and Mary II.*

OPPOSITE: *Mary II only reigned for five years, from 1689–94. She was the daughter of James II, whom she and her husband, William III, deposed.*

In July 1981, Prince Charles was the focus of world attention when he married Lady Diana Spencer at St Paul's. Taking place in a summer that had been marred by serious riots in Bristol, the wedding captured the imagination not only of Britain, but of the world – 750 million people watched the service on television. The cathedral was also the venue for services to celebrate the 80th and 100th birthdays of Queen Elizabeth, the Queen Mother, in 1980 and 2000 respectively. On 4 June 2002, Queen Elizabeth II and the Duke of Edinburgh attended a Golden Jubilee service at St Paul's, having travelled here in the Gold State Coach.

QUEENHITHE
EC4

This is one of the ancient quays that punctuate the banks of the River Thames: they have long since lost that original function. Before the 12th century, London residents called this quay Ethelredshythe, after the Alderman of Mercia, who was the son-in-law of King Alfred. However, its name was changed in honour of Queen Matilda (1080–1118), the wife of Henry I, who built the first public lavatory here in the early 12th century. There was an announcement that the lavatory was for 'the common use of the citizens', which was a revolutionary idea at the time.

After Matilda's great-grandson, King John (1199–1216), succeeded to the throne, he gave the quay to his mother, Eleanor of Aquitaine (c. 1122–1204). She collected customs tolls here in such an exacting fashion that she made herself extremely unpopular. Ownership of Queenhithe passed to each ruling queen in turn, and by the 15th century, it had become the most important of the London docks. However, it had reached its zenith, because by this time the boats had become too large to dock in this small medieval quay, and their owners preferred to berth in nearby Billingsgate. This had the added advantage of being downstream from London Bridge, so boats were spared the tricky business of navigating their way through its arches and the dangerous currents that these created.

WILLIAMSON'S TAVERN
Groveland Court, Bow Lane, EC4

This old inn has a fascinating history. It was built on the site of a house owned by Sir John Falstaff and some authorities claim that the new building was the original official residence of the Lord Mayor of London before the Mansion House was built in the first half of the 18th century. On one occasion, the Lord Mayor gave a dinner here for William III and Mary II, who presented him with a pair of wrought-iron gates. The story goes that the mayor accepted the gates, but then ordered that they should be taken outside, which incensed Mary so much that she insisted they were brought inside again. They now have a permanent resting place outside, and can still be seen at the end of the alley.

The building was bought by Robert Williamson in 1739, which is the year when the foundation stone for the present Mansion House at Bank was laid. Williamson turned the house into a tavern, naming it after himself. Many modern pubs have various machines that can entertain the clientele, but Williamson's Tavern has the distinction of containing a stone that marks the centre of the City of London.

THE CHURCH OF ST MARY-LE-BOW
Bow Lane, EC2

Any child born within the sound of Bow bells can claim to be a true Cockney. The Bow bells in question belong to those of the church of St Mary-le-Bow, although today it is a wonder that they can be heard at all above the rumble of the traffic in Cheapside.

The church, which dates from Norman times, was originally called Sancta Marie de Arcubus, because of the arches (or bows) that can still be seen in the crypt. The earliest mention of the church dates from 1091 when it lost its roof during a storm. Some unfortunate incidents took place in the church: 20 people died when the tower collapsed in 1271, and a goldsmith was murdered here in 1284, after which the church had to be re-consecrated. In 1331, a joust was held to celebrate the birth of Edward of Woodstock (1330–76), the eldest son of Edward III. He later became known as the Black Prince because of the colour of his armour. His mother, Philippa of Hainault (*c.* 1314–69), was watching the entertainment from a wooden balcony with her ladies-in-waiting when it collapsed under them. They survived, and the rebuilt balcony continued to be used by other monarchs who enjoyed watching City pageants from its lofty position.

The church was one of the casualties during the Great Fire in 1666, and was rebuilt in 1670–73 by Sir Christopher Wren, who based his design on the Basilica of Maxentius in Rome. He retained the balcony, in memory of the dramatic incident of 1331, and it was from here that Queen Anne watched the Lord Mayor's procession in 1702, the same year that she succeeded to the throne. Luckily for her, the balcony remained securely in place.

ABOVE: *The original 1708 figures of the giants Gog and Magog were destroyed in 1940 but have now been replaced by copies in limewood.*

ST LAWRENCE JEWRY
Gresham Street, EC2

Edward I was not a tolerant man. He reigned from 1272–1307, during which time he quelled a number of uprisings in Scotland and Wales, thereby displaying his tremendous gifts as a military tactician. In 1291, Edward was responsible for the violent expulsion of the Jewish community living in this area of London. They occupied a site that centred around Old Jewry, which allowed them to retain an independent community, but it also left them vulnerable to attack by anyone who took against them. The Crown made them pay extortionate taxes and they were also scapegoats for many anti-Semitic fears. Finally, the Jewish people of the area were expelled by Edward, who showed no mercy in his treatment of them. He subsequently acquired their property, which he sold for a healthy profit.

The church of St Lawrence Jewry, first built in 1136, stood on the fringe of this Jewish ghetto, hence its name. It was dedicated to St Lawrence, who was roasted alive on a gridiron in the 3rd century AD. Sir Thomas More (1478–1535), who fell foul of Henry VIII and was eventually executed on his orders, once preached at this church.

St Lawrence Jewry was destroyed during the Great Fire of London in 1666, but it was rebuilt by Sir Christopher Wren between 1671–77. Wren's great patron, Charles II, was present at the re-dedication ceremony. Only the walls and tower were left standing after the church was badly bombed during the Blitz in 1940, but it was rebuilt by Cecil Brown between 1954–57 to Wren's original designs. St Lawrence Jewry has been the official church of the Corporation of London since 1822, when the Guildhall Chapel was demolished.

GUILDHALL
EC2

Guildhall is the administrative headquarters of the Corporation of the City of London and has therefore been of great importance ever since the present building was erected in 1411. Its size is an indication of its significance, as it is the third largest hall in England after Westminster Hall and the Great Hall of the Archbishop's Palace in Canterbury. Lord Mayors and Sheriffs were elected in Guildhall, and the Court of Common Council (the governing body of the City of London, led by the Lord Mayor) met here.

The Nine-Day Queen

In medieval London, important trials were also held at Guildhall. One of the most notable occurred in 1553, when Lady Jane Grey and her husband, Lord Guilford Dudley, were tried for treason. Lady Jane was the granddaughter of Henry VIII's sister Mary, Duchess of Suffolk, and therefore the king's great-niece. When Henry died in 1547, his will stated that the line of succession should pass in the following order – to his son, Edward; his daughter, Mary; his second daughter, Elizabeth; their heirs; and then to the heirs of his sister, Mary. Edward VI duly

inherited the throne, but he was only nine and so John Dudley, Duke of Northumberland, was appointed Lord Protector. When Edward, always a sickly child, lay dying in 1553, Northumberland saw this as a chance to continue his power and to ensure the success of the newly established Protestant religion. He therefore persuaded the young king to change his father's will. Mary was barred from the succession on the grounds of her Catholicism and Elizabeth was barred because she had not stated her religious convictions, so the crown conveniently passed to Lady Jane Grey – who just happened to be Northumberland's daughter-in-law. Northumberland had ensured this connection by hastily marrying his son, Guilford, to Jane in May 1553, a few weeks before the death of Edward VI. Lady Jane reigned for nine days before being deposed by Mary I on 19 July 1553. Lady Jane and her husband were found guilty of treason, and both were executed on Tower Hill in February 1554. Archbishop Cranmer (1489–1556), who was one of the many people who countersigned Edward VI's will, was also hauled off to Guildhall where he was tried and found guilty of treason, and burnt at the stake.

Statues by Nicholas Stone of Edward VI, Elizabeth I and Charles I once stood in the adjoining Guildhall Chapel, but when this was demolished in 1822 they were moved to their present position on the staircase to the old library in Guildhall.

THE CLOCKMAKERS' COMPANY MUSEUM
Aldermanbury, EC2

London is full of interesting little corners and places that deserve a second look, and this is definitely one of them. As its name suggests, this is the museum of the Worshipful Company of Clockmakers, which was founded in 1631. It can be found in the public library next to Guildhall (see page 48), which is appropriate because the members of the guild have always worked close to Guildhall.

The museum contains a skull watch that was believed to have been given to a maid-of-honour by Mary, Queen of Scots (1542–67). It also displays the H5 chronometer, which was one of the marine timepieces that John Harrison (1693–1776) developed in order to find a sure means of measuring longitude at sea. The H5 was tested by George III, who was fascinated by science and scientific apparatus.

Aldermanbury also has an interesting history, because it is believed to have been the site of a royal castle that stood here long before Edward the Confessor built his palace at Westminster in 1060. One of its residents may have been Ethelbert, the King of Kent between 560–616. Aldermanbury means 'alderman's manor' and dates from the 14th century, when the alderman in question may have been Ethelred, the son-in-law of Alfred the Great.

BELOW: *'The Old Lady of Threadneedle Street', as the Bank of England is popularly known, was founded with the permission of William III.*

THE BANK OF ENGLAND
Threadneedle Street, EC2

It took a Dutchman to create the Bank of England. When William III, the Prince of Orange, sailed from the Netherlands to Britain to take the throne in 1688, he did so thanks to a loan from a Sephardic Jew, Francisco Lopez Suasso. A few years later, in 1694, William was attempting to raise sufficient money to fund a war with France. Two City merchants, William Patterson and Michael Godfrey, suggested that a national bank should be founded, which could then loan the necessary money to the government. William agreed, taking the structure of the Bank of Amsterdam as his inspiration.

The Bank of England was incorporated by Royal Charter on 27 July 1694 and was an instant success. The bank began trading at Mercers' Hall, Cheapside, but moved to the Grocer's Hall in Princes Street a few months later, where it stayed until 1734 when it moved to its present site.

One of the functions of the bank is to issue banknotes and coins. The coins have always been stamped with a portrait of the head of the reigning monarch, although banknotes did not carry a portrait of the sovereign until 1960.

THE ROYAL EXCHANGE
Threadneedle Street at Royal Exchange Buildings, EC3

The Royal Exchange stood on this spot between 1566–1939. It began life when Thomas Gresham, a successful London trader who owned a shop in nearby Lombard Street, recognized the need for a meeting place in which merchants and adventurers could conduct business with each other. Gresham laid the first brick in June 1566 and the building was ready by the winter of 1567. Statues of English monarchs were set in niches overlooking the court-

ABOVE: *For centuries, the accession to the throne of a new sovereign was proclaimed from the steps leading up to the Royal Exchange.*

yard, but Nicholas Stone's statue of Elizabeth I was deemed unsuitable and was moved to the Guildhall Chapel; it now stands on the staircase leading to the old library in Guildhall (see page 48).

When Elizabeth I visited what was then called the Exchange in January 1570, an accompanying herald proclaimed that it was henceforth to be known as the Royal Exchange. It was one of the many buildings destroyed during the Great Fire of London in 1666, but it was quickly rebuilt. A further collection of statues of monarchs graced the courtyard, and more were added until the reign of George IV. In January 1838, fire once again destroyed the Royal Exchange and many of the royal statues were sold at auction that April. The third building was completed in 1844 and was opened by Queen Victoria, who followed the tradition set by her ancestor, Elizabeth I, and proclaimed that the building should henceforth be called the Royal Exchange. More royal statues appeared, including those of Victoria, Prince Albert and Elizabeth I.

Such was the importance of the Royal Exchange that it was one of the places in London where a new sovereign was proclaimed. Today, however, it has been developed into a complex of expensive shops and is therefore fulfilling a different function for Londoners.

THE MONUMENT
Monument Street and Fish Street Hill, EC2

Just before 2am on 2 September 1666, during what was proving to be a very hot and dry summer, a small fire started in a bakery in Pudding Lane. The business was owned by a royal baker named Robert Farriner, who led his family across the rooftops, away from the blaze and to safety. At first, despite a strong wind that was fanning the flames, the fire was not taken seriously. When the Lord Mayor, Sir Thomas Bloodworth, was woken up to be given the news, he airily dismissed it: 'Pish! A woman might piss it out!'

Royalty Rallies Round
However, the fire quickly took hold and by the time the diarist Samuel Pepys (1633–1703) visited Charles II and his brother, James, Duke of York, at Whitehall later that morning, over 300 houses and half of London Bridge had been reduced to ash. Charles II told Pepys to instruct the Lord Mayor to pull down houses in order to create a fire break, but when Pepys carried out his commission he was told that the fire was spreading too quickly for this to be effective. The Duke of York was put in charge of fighting the fire, and Charles II helped soldiers attack the blaze, but the flames still raged out of control. The fire finally ended five days after it had started, by which time it had burned 400 acres (162 hectares) within the city walls and 63 acres (25.5 hectares) beyond

them, destroying nearly 14,000 homes and 87 churches. It had also fumigated a city that was still recovering from the ghastly effects of the Great Plague the summer before. Homeless Londoners camped out in fields and were visited by Charles II on horseback, who promised that they would be fed and reassured them that the fire was not the result of a foreign or Catholic plot. Nevertheless, a Huguenot called Robert Hubert confessed to the fire (even though he was almost undoubtedly innocent), thereby offering himself as a convenient foreign scapegoat.

BELOW: *The panels around the base of the Monument commemorate the dramatic story of the Great Fire of London in 1666.*

Rebuilding the City

When an Act of Parliament was passed about the rebuilding of London, it also ruled that a monument to the fire should be erected. It was designed, like so much else in London in the second half of the 17th century, by Sir Christopher Wren, in conjunction with his friend, Robert Hooke. It stands 202 feet (61 metres) high, which is the distance between the monument and the baker's shop in Pudding Lane, and is the tallest isolated stone column in the world. A series of panels around its base records the events of September 1666 and also notes the part played by Charles II in London's reconstruction. He saw this as an opportunity to build a properly planned city, rather than to reproduce the confusing network of narrow streets that had existed before the fire. Another panel, created by Caius Gabriel Cibber (1630–1700), shows Charles and his brother conducting the fire-fighting operations.

There is an unpleasant postscript to this story. In 1681, the inscription on one of the panels describing the progress of the fire received an addition, which read 'But Popish frenzy, which wrought such horrors, is not yet quenched.' Seven years later, anti-Catholic sentiment forced James II off the throne. This addition was finally removed in 1831.

LONDON BRIDGE
EC4, SE1

This is one of the most famous bridges in the world, even though the present structure, which was built in 1972, hardly merits such an accolade. Actually, it is the history of London Bridge that is so thrilling. We remember it in the nursery rhyme, 'London Bridge is falling down', even if we do not know exactly what it refers to.

In fact, the nursery rhyme commemorates one of the earliest incidents in the long history of the bridge. In 994, London was attacked by Olaf Tryggvason of Norway and Sweyn Forkbeard of Denmark, who managed to extract large amounts of money, or 'danegeld', from the city during the following 20 years. Ethelred II (978–1016), who was King of England at the time, was unable to stand up to this aggressive treatment and was usurped by Sweyn Forkbeard in 1013. Sweyn was never crowned and died in 1014, allowing Ethelred to take back the English throne. That same year, Ethelred joined forces with King Olaf of Norway to repel the Danes, and succeeded by burning down the wooden London Bridge while the Danes

ABOVE: *This is the 19th-century London Bridge that replaced the celebrated medieval bridge.*

were on it. This was celebrated by a Norse poet named Ottar Svarte and his poem was adapted in the 17th century to the version we know now.

The Medieval Bridge

The first stone bridge across the Thames at this point was erected in the 1170s and the first houses were built on it a few years later. In the centre of the bridge was a chapel dedicated to St Thomas Becket, who had been murdered in Canterbury Cathedral by supporters of Henry II (1154–89).

During the Baron's War in 1264, Henry III was taken prisoner by Simon de Montfort (*c.* 1208–65). When de Montfort tried to cross London Bridge with his royal prisoner, the Lord Mayor pulled up the drawbridge and locked the gates. However, Londoners then knocked down the gates to let de Montfort into the city.

One of the more colourful traditions of medieval London involved beheading prisoners, boiling their heads in tar to preserve them, and then sticking these on poles above the bridge's gatehouse. Edward II's great Scots enemy, William Wallace, who was executed at Smithfield (see page 43), was the first man whose head was treated in this way. Sir Thomas More, who was Henry VIII's trusted adviser before he so offended the king by refusing to agree to his divorce from Katherine of Aragon, was also beheaded and his head was impaled above the gatehouse in 1535. Five years on, Thomas Cromwell (*c.* 1485–1540), who had supported More's execution, received exactly the same treatment.

London Bridge was also the setting for happier events. When Henry V returned victorious from the Battle of Agincourt in France in 1415, he rode over the bridge with the Lord Mayor. Upon his restoration to the throne in 1660, Charles II rode into London over the bridge accompanied by a massive retinue.

Footpads and Frost Fairs

London Bridge was the only structure to span the Thames until 1738, when work began on Westminster Bridge, which was completed in 1750. This was followed by Blackfriars Bridge, which was built in 1760–69. London Bridge was long considered a dangerous haunt of footpads (robbers) and other insalubrious characters, and Elizabeth I, among others, refused to cross it,

always using a ferry instead. However, London Bridge did have something to recommend it, because its many piers slowed the flow of the river to such an extent that the Thames often froze hard from bank to bank in winter. This is the reason for the many frost fairs that took place on the Thames during bitter winters. In 1683, Charles II visited that winter's frost fair and, along with many other Londoners, bought a certificate with his name printed on it to testify to his attendance. The last frost fair was held in the winter of 1813.

London Bridge, Arizona

The 19th century saw the end of the medieval London Bridge, with a replacement built upstream by Sir John Rennie (1794–1874) between 1823–31. The bridge was opened on 1 August

1831 by William IV and Queen Adelaide and one of its approach roads, King William Street, was named after the monarch. This bridge was replaced by the current structure in 1972. The old bridge was sold for $2.4 million and re-erected in Lake Havasu City, Arizona. Popular gossip at the time speculated that the purchasers had confused their London bridges and thought they were buying the much more interesting Tower Bridge.

THE TOWER OF LONDON
Tower Hill, EC3

One of the most celebrated and distinctive buildings in the world, the Tower of London occupies a majestic position on the banks of the Thames just outside the City of London. For centuries, the sight of its rising towers and thick walls struck terror in the hearts of many Londoners because the Tower was a fortified prison as well as a royal palace. Many royal personages were held against their will here, and two kings are believed to have been murdered within its walls. The Tower was also a place of official execution for those of noble birth, and it was where three queens of England were beheaded. Other prisoners were executed in public on Tower Hill, outside the fortress's walls.

A Norman Conquest
From its earliest days, when Norman builders started to construct the castle's keep, soon after William the Conqueror had successfully invaded England in 1066, the main purposes of the Tower of London were subjugation and control. The new

ABOVE: *The Crown Jewels are held within the Tower in conditions of the greatest security.*

OPPOSITE: *Katherine Howard was executed on Tower Green only 18 months after becoming queen.*

regime knew it had to keep strict control of its conquered people, despite William's assurances that he would be 'a gracious liege Lord' to the English. Blood had already been spilt at William's coronation on Christmas Day 1066, when Norman soldiers misinterpreted the watching crowd's hurrahs as cries of defiance and promptly killed them. This was not the most auspicious beginning to William's reign, yet he wanted to ensure that the English people understood that he and his men would not hesitate to quell any insurrection.

William died in 1087 and his son and successor, the highly unpopular William II (called William Rufus because of his red hair), continued the building project that had been started by his father. The keep was completed during his reign. In 1240, it was whitewashed, after which it became known as the White Tower. Successive kings added to the complex of buildings within the fortress as the need arose. During the 13th and 14th centuries, the outer wall, the inner curtain wall and the moat were created. Such powerful defensive structures were needed to combat the constant threat of uprisings from malcontents and pretenders to the throne. As the centuries progressed, the buildings within the Tower were adapted, enlarged or demolished and replaced, according to the needs and styles of the period and the whims of the reigning monarch.

Royal Residents

One of the main requirements of the Tower of London was to serve as a royal palace; its secure fortifications were a necessary precaution in medieval England where the threat of plague, revolt and other trouble was never far away. The Tower's first royal resident was King Stephen (1135–54), who stayed here at Whitsun 1140. In January 1236, the newly married Henry III accompanied his bride, Eleanor of Provence, from the Tower to her coronation in Westminster Abbey. This was the first time that the coronation procession started from the Tower, where the royal couple had stayed the night before, and it set a precedent that continued until 1604, when James I was the last monarch to spend his pre-coronation night at the Tower. By this time, the buildings were in such a bad state that the castle was not considered a safe or comfortable place in which a monarch should sleep. However, Charles II paid lip-service to this old tradition at his coronation in April 1661 when the royal procession rode to the gates of the Tower at dawn, so it could at least be seen to start from here.

A Bloody History

Although the Tower has served many purposes in its existence, including providing a home for the Royal Menagerie, the Royal Mint and the Crown Jewels, two of its most colourful and notorious functions were as a prison for royalty and a place of execution. In 1241–44, the Tower was the prison of Llywelyn ap Gruffydd, who was the Welsh Prince of Wales (the English did not appoint their own Prince of Wales until 1301, when the infant Prince Edward, son of Edward I, was given this title). He fell to his death while trying to escape from the Tower. Richard II was the first English king to be imprisoned in the Tower in 1399, and he was forced to abdicate during his stay. James I of Scotland (1406–37) was locked in the Tower in 1406, having been abducted on his way to France. On 21 May 1471, Henry VI was murdered in the Tower while he was at prayer. It is alleged that his murderer was the Duke of Gloucester – the future Richard III – who is also believed to have dispatched Edward V and his brother, Richard, Duke of York, in the Tower in 1483. Princess Elizabeth was imprisoned in the Tower by her half-sister, Mary I, in 1554, but was released and lived to become Elizabeth I.

In addition to all these royal prisoners, three official executions of queens were carried out on Tower Green within the walls of the castle. Anne Boleyn, the second wife of Henry VIII, was executed on 19 May 1536; Henry's fifth wife, Katherine Howard, suffered the same fate on 13 February 1542; and Lady Jane Grey, who was queen so briefly in July 1553, was executed on 12 February 1554. They, and the four other people who are known to have been beheaded on Tower Green, were buried in the Chapel of St Peter ad Vincula, which stands nearby.

The Crown Jewels
The Tower is known worldwide as the home of the English Crown Jewels, which have been on public display since the 17th century. Most of the collection is known as the Coronation Regalia, as it is used in coronations, and includes the Orb and Sceptre that were made for Charles II's coronation in 1661, after the restoration of the monarchy the previous year. Most of the Coronation Regalia dates from this time, as it replaced the regalia that was melted down after the execution of Charles I, when

Britain was briefly a republic under the rule of Oliver Cromwell. Later additions to the Coronation Regalia include St Edward's Crown, which was made in 1661 for Charles II, and the Imperial State Crown, which was worn by George VI at his coronation in 1937 and, after re-modelling, by his daughter, Elizabeth II, in 1953.

It is tempting to imagine that the Tower is a series of buildings that now function as little more than a busy tourist attraction. In fact, the Tower is still a fortress that is protected by Yeomen Warders round the clock, ending each day with the highly atmospheric Ceremony of the Keys in which the outer gates are locked for the night.

STATUE OF QUEEN ALEXANDRA
Royal London Hospital, Whitechapel Road, E1

This hospital was founded in 1740, at which point it was known as the London Infirmary and was situated in Prescot Street. It changed its name to the London Hospital in 1748, and then moved to its present position, surrounded by what were then green fields, in 1753. The hospital grew in size, and, in 1867 Queen Victoria opened a new wing, which made it the largest hospital in Britain. In July 1990, it became the Royal London Hospital, when Queen Elizabeth II visited it to commemorate its 250th anniversary.

The bronze statue of Queen Alexandra is by George Edward Wade and was cast in 1908. It shows the queen in her coronation robes and the inscription explains that she 'introduced to England the Finsen Light cure for lupus and presented the first lamp to this hospital'. This is just one example of her charitable work because Alexandra was a very conscientious Queen Consort. She had particular sympathy with people who were ill because she suffered from a series of health problems herself, including deafness and lameness. Her mother-in-law, Queen Victoria, once wrote of her that she was 'one of those sweet creatures who seem to come from the skies to help and bless mortals'.

Chapter 3

PICCADILLY TO HACKNEY

This section of London incorporates parts of the West End as well as corners of the City of London. The Strand runs through it like a long spine, connecting secular sites, such as Somerset House, with sacred places like the church of St Bride. There is also a theatre with two royal boxes that were constructed after George III and the Prince Regent had a row in the foyer, and a police station where the colour of the outside lamp was altered because of Queen Victoria's dislike of anything blue.

LEFT: *The clock tower of St Anne's church gives an idea of how the rest of the building looked when George, Prince of Wales was a parishioner.*

OPPOSITE: *Somerset House is one of the most beautiful Georgian buildings in London. It replaced the original Renaissance palace.*

ABOVE: *The tomb of Theodore, once the King of Corsica, lies at the base of the tower of St Anne's, which is all that remains of the old church.*

QUEEN STREET
Mayfair, W1

Queen Street lies between Charles Street and Curzon Street, in a very exclusive part of Mayfair. William IV lived at 22 Charles Street for a short time in 1826, when he was the Duke of Clarence, and many other illustrious people lived around here in the 19th century.

However, scandal surrounded the occupants of 6 Queen Street, because it was the home of a grandson of George III, George, Duke of Cambridge (1819–1904), and his actress wife, Sarah Fairbrother, who became known as Mrs Fitzgeorge. They were married privately in January 1847, in contravention of the Royal Marriages Act of 1772 – in other words, without the consent of the reigning monarch, Queen Victoria. They had three children, although the first two were born before their marriage, which must have been even

more shocking at the time. Queen Victoria would definitely not have been amused. Mrs Fitzgeorge died at 6 Queen Street in January 1890.

The duke's grandfather, George III, is alleged to have contracted his own unsuitable marriage in April 1759 to Hannah Lightfoot, the daughter of a cobbler from Wapping, by whom he is rumoured to have had three children. If this is true, his official marriage to Charlotte Mecklenburg-Strelitz in 1761 is bigamous, and all his descendants have no claim to the British throne. Ironically, it was George III who introduced the Royal Marriages Act of 1772, expressly to stop members of the Royal Family from making unfortunate marriages.

ST JAMES'S CHURCH
Piccadilly, W1

This is one of the few churches that Sir Christopher Wren built outside the City of London, and the only one not to stand on the site of a previous church. Instead, it was built between 1676–84 on land acquired by Henry Jermyn, Earl of St Albans, on what had once been part of St James's Fields, next to St James's Palace. Wren was delighted with the church, particularly its acoustics.

St James quickly became a fashionable place of worship, no doubt helped by its proximity to St James's Palace. The organ was built by Renatus Harris and was made for the Chapel Royal in Whitehall in 1685, when James II was on the throne. In 1691, James's daughter, Mary II, was asked by the rector, Dr Thomas Tenison (1636–1715), to give the organ to St James's. After it was installed in the church it was tested by both John Blow (1648–78) and Henry Purcell (*c.* 1659–95). Grinling Gibbons designed the organ case.

St James's Church was badly damaged during the Second World War and re-dedicated in 1954. The churchyard was turned into a garden of remembrance, in honour of the courage of Londoners during the Blitz, and was opened by Queen Mary in 1946. It is now the venue for a daily craft market.

ST ANNE'S CHURCH
Wardour Street, W1

This church is one of London's many curiosities. Only the tower remains from the original building, as the rest of the church was destroyed during an air raid in 1940. St Anne's was built between

1677–86 by the architect William Talman and it quickly gained a royal parishioner in the Prince of Wales (later George II), who had 'an Inclination to come to this church'. St Anne's has another royal connection. Theodore, the dethroned King of Corsica, was buried here in 1756 and his epitaph was written by Horace Walpole.

Passers-by may wonder why the gardens of the church are so high. This is because they were consistently raised in order to accommodate the 10,000 bodies of parishioners who lie underneath them.

SOHO SQUARE
W1

In the days of Henry VIII, long before London was covered by concrete and high-rise buildings, the area around what we now know as Soho was used for hunting. Various calls were used during hunts, one of which was 'So Ho'. It became the rallying cry of Charles II's illegitimate son, the Duke of Monmouth (1649–85), at the Battle of Sedgemoor in 1685.

Monmouth knew this area of London well. In the 1660s, his father had given him the land around what is now Soho Square. He built an aptly impressive mansion on the site called Monmouth House.

The square was laid out in the 1680s, and was initially called King Square in honour of Charles II; a stone statue of the monarch, which was fashioned by Caius Gabriel Cibber, stood in the garden at the centre. Thanks to the hard work of Richard Frith, the bricklayer who gave his name to nearby Frith Street, the square contained a total of 41 houses by 1691, including Monmouth's own residence. The area quickly became a very fashionable address and attracted various very important people.

In the 1870s, the statue of Charles II was removed and replaced by the mock-Tudor shed that still stands here. The statue was given a new home at Grimsdyke House in Harrow, where it stayed in private ownership (its last owner was the librettist, W.S. Gilbert) until it was returned to the square in 1938.

NATIONAL PORTRAIT GALLERY
St Martin's Place, WC2

If you want to view portraits of virtually every monarch from Richard III to Elizabeth II and her immediate family, this is the place to come. The portraits are arranged chronologically and are a fascinating insight into the kings and queens of Britain because they tell us so much about them. A wily Henry VII looks sideways at us, a Lancastrian red rose in his hand as a reminder of his rather shaky claim to be the rightful heir to the throne through the House of Lancaster. History tells us that he was mean with money, and a quick glance at his pinched face seems to confirm this. Charles I, painted by Daniel Mytens in 1631, stares straight ahead, appearing slightly hesitant but the essence of romantic innocence; 18 years later he was executed after losing a power struggle with Parliament. The heavily lined face of his son, Charles II, in a portrait painted by John Michael Wright or his studio in the 1660s, is the epitome of world-weary dissipation. He was only in his early 30s, but it is evident that he had packed a tremendous amount into those years.

There are many photographs, too, which date from the Victorian age onwards. Queen Victoria is pictured with John Brown and later Abdul Karim (known as her Munshi), the two

BELOW: *Prince Albert helped to set up the National Portrait Gallery, which is a treasure trove of royal portraits and photographs.*

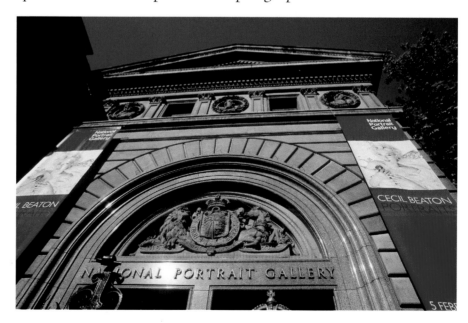

notorious servants who won her affections and caused scandal in the process.

The National Portrait Gallery even had a royal backer in Prince Albert, who in 1856 approved the suggestion of Philip, 5th Earl of Stanhope, that there should be 'a gallery of the portraits of the most eminent persons in British history'. When it opened in 1859, the gallery had 57 portraits; today, it has over 9,000 in its collection.

ST GILES-IN-THE-FIELDS
St Giles, WC2

St Giles is the patron saint of outcasts, which gives a clue about the name of this church and the original nature of this area. The land once comprised fields that stood outside the city wall. In 1101, it became the site of a leper hospital founded by Matilda, wife of Henry I. It was a miserable place, not just because of the lepers, but because prisoners from Newgate passed by the hospital chapel on their way to be executed at Tyburn.

The chapel soon became a place of worship for parishioners as well as patients, and it continued as a church even after Henry VIII closed the hospital in 1539. Another church was built on the site in 1623, but it had to be rebuilt the following century, as the foundations had been undermined by the extraordinary number of burials in the churchyard. The new church was built by Henry Flitcroft (1687–1769), the son of William III's gardener, and was completed in 1733. Nearby Flitcroft Street is named after the church's architect.

St Giles was a highly insalubrious district for centuries – it was the setting for William Hogarth's illustration, *Gin Lane*, and Byron described the area as one of 'squalid wretchedness' – which is why the church had no royal visitors or patrons after the saintly Matilda. Nevertheless, there are some royal connections. Catherine Sedley, an unpopular mistress of James II, was baptized here in 1657. There is also a tombstone bearing the name of Richard Penderel, one of four brothers who risked their lives after the Battle of Worcester by hiding the fugitive Charles II in an oak tree at Boscobel, Shropshire.

TRAFALGAR SQUARE
WC2, SW1

Today, despite the efforts of the London Mayor to discourage them, Trafalgar Square is overrun with pigeons. They are part of the square's character and are a direct avian link with its original purpose. During the medieval period, the area we now know as Trafalgar Square was the King's Mews and home of the royal falcons. The poet Geoffrey Chaucer (1344–1400) was, at one point, Clerk of the Mews.

The royal mews had vanished by the time Henry VII came to the throne in the 15th century and was replaced by the royal stables. These burned down in 1534, while Henry VIII was on the throne, but they were rebuilt by his daughter, Elizabeth I. During the English Civil War in the 1640s, the stables were initially turned into barracks for the Parliamentary army. They were subsequently converted into a prison for 4,500 Royalists who had been captured at the Battle of Naseby in 1645.

Following the Restoration in 1660, there were grand plans for Sir Christopher Wren to rebuild the stables; however, these did not materialize. Instead William Kent rebuilt the main stable block in 1732, on the site now occupied by the National Gallery.

The site was redeveloped during the reign of George IV, and the National Gallery was founded in 1824. The Corinthian columns supporting the portico of the main entrance were taken from George IV's private London residence, Carlton House, when it was demolished to help finance the building work at Buckingham Palace.

STATUE OF CHARLES I
Trafalgar Square, WC1

Marooned on a traffic island to the south of Trafalgar Square, a bronze equestrian statue of Charles I stares down Whitehall towards the scene of his execution, which took place on 30 January 1649, outside the Banqueting House (see page 33). You might take your life in your hands by trying to dodge the buses and taxis in order to inspect the statue at close range, but it's worth it because there are three fascinating stories connected with it.

Statue Stories
The statue was cast in bronze by Hubert Le Sueur (*c.* 1595–1650) in 1632, and was commissioned by Lord Weston, High Treasurer, who intended to erect it in his garden at Roehampton. However, trouble was already brewing for Charles I and it

OPPOSITE: *The bronze statue of Charles I has had an extraordinary history, being stashed away in a Covent Garden crypt during the Civil War.*

was considered politic to hide the statue. Royalists stashed it away in the crypt of St Paul's Church, Covent Garden, where it was discovered by the Parliamentarians in 1655. The Civil War was still raging, and a brass-worker from Holborn, named John Rivett, was instructed to melt down the statue. Instead, he hid it while making a tidy sum from selling pieces of what was alleged to be the statue of the 'late king and martyr'. After the Restoration in 1660, Rivett refused to give the statue to Weston's son. Nevertheless, Charles II eventually acquired it and it was finally erected at its present site in 1676. The choice of site was no accident: it marks the place where eight of

the regicides and signatories to Charles I's death warrant were disembowelled in 1660.

The site is important for another reason, as the original Charing Cross stood here until 1647. This was the last of the series of stone crosses erected by Edward I to mark the resting places of the funeral cortège of his first wife, Eleanor (c. 1244–90), when her body was brought back to Westminster from Nottinghamshire in 1291. A Victorian replica of the stone cross now stands outside Charing Cross station, from which it got its name.

As if all that was not enough, the statue of Charles I has a third significance: it stands at the point from which all distances to London are calculated.

ST MARTIN-IN-THE-FIELDS
Trafalgar Square, WC2

This is the parish church of Buckingham Palace and in the 1700s it even had a king – George I – as its churchwarden. He was the only reigning monarch ever to have been given such a post, and it seems that he was not very assiduous at the task because he rarely put in an appearance. By way of compensation, he donated an organ to the church. George's Royal Arms adorn the pediment above the Corinthian columns of the entrance and his portrait hangs in the south-west porch.

There are many royal connections with St Martin-in-the-Fields. The original Norman church was pulled down and rebuilt by Henry VIII around 1542. A new chancel was built between 1606–09 and paid for by Prince Henry (1594–1612), the eldest son of James I. St Martin-in-the-Fields was the church in which the infant Prince Charles, later Charles II, was christened in 1630. One of Charles's most famous and popular mistresses, Nell Gwyn, was buried in the churchyard in 1687.

The church was once again pulled down and rebuilt in 1722–26. It was designed by James Gibbs, who initially wanted to make the building circular. However, he had to alter his plans to fit in with the strict budget imposed by the Commissioners for the Building of Fifty New Churches. His eventual design – a large, rectangular church with a portico and a tall steeple – was much imitated in New England.

Inside the church, the Royal Box is on the left of the high altar and the Admiralty Box (the Admiralty in Whitehall is contained within the parish) is on the right. The Royal Arms from 1725 are situated on the arch above the altar.

STATUE OF GEORGE III
Cockspur Street, SW1

George III eventually died in 1820, having suffered for many years from what we now know to be porphyria, but which was considered to be insanity at the time. A public subscription was set up that same year to raise the funds for a statue of the late king, which was installed in

OPPOSITE: *Mary I is one of the monarchs who used to worship at St Martin-in-the-Fields. She gave some tapestries to the church.*

Cockspur Street in 1836. The finished article was a bronze equestrian statue by Matthew Cotes Wyatt (1777–1862) with the horse's tail raised horizontally. This led to a popular verse of the time:

Here stands a statue at which critics rail
To point a moral and to point a Tail.

COUTTS & CO
The Strand, WC1

Characterized by its oversized chequebooks, Coutts is one of the oldest banks to survive in London. It was founded in 1692 by a Scottish goldsmith called John Campbell, and situated at 'the sign of The Three Crowns in the Strand'. This was a peculiarly apt address, considering the bank's later list of royal clients.

Royal Accounts
The first of these arrived in 1716, when the future George II bought some silver plate. The bank flourished, attracting many important political and aristocratic clients over the following years, including George III who opened an account with them. Since then, every succeeding sovereign has had a bank account with Coutts. There is even a Coutts ATM (automatic teller machine) in the basement of Buckingham Palace for the staff to use. The bank is no longer privately owned, as it is now part of the Royal Bank of Scotland, but it is still considered to be very prestigious. Until 1993, Coutts sent a horse-drawn carriage to deliver royal correspondence, but unfortunately that tradition has now ended.

There is a fascinating royal story connected with Coutts. In 1917, during the First World War, the parents of Elizabeth Bowes-Lyon, later Queen Elizabeth the Queen Mother, discovered that their son, Michael, was still alive through a Coutts cheque. He had been declared missing in action on the Western Front and his family feared that he had suffered the same fate as his brother, Fergus, who had been killed. In fact, Michael was a prisoner of war in Germany, and he succeeded in drawing some money from his captors by writing them a cheque. When the cheque was presented at Coutts, the manager rang the Bowes-Lyon family to give them the good news.

SAVOY CHAPEL
Savoy Street, WC2

Centuries before this corner of London was covered by the luxurious Savoy Hotel, it was the site of the Savoy Palace, which was owned by one of Edward III's sons, John of Gaunt, Duke of Lancaster (1340–99). The palace had an accompanying chapel, dedicated to St John the Baptist, but both chapel and palace were destroyed during the Peasants' Revolt of 1381. The buildings lay in ruins until 1505 when Henry VII announced that a hospital for the poor should be built here, once again dedicated to St John the Baptist. It had three chapels, including the Savoy Chapel, which is now all that remains of the medieval palace. The chapel is a royal peculiar, which means that it is privately owned by the reigning sovereign in his or her role as the Duke of Lancaster.

The 16th century was a tumultuous time, thanks to the many disputes about the national religion, and all religious institutions suffered the consequences of these arguments. The hospital was no exception. It was closed down by Edward VI (1547–53) in 1553, only to be opened again by his half-sister, Mary I, three years later. However, the hospital soon fell into disrepute, with claims that it was the 'chief nurserie of evil men', as criminals took refuge from the law there. In the 17th century, it became first a barracks for Foot Guards and then a Jesuit school. After a disastrous fire in 1776, the site was cleared in 1816–20 and redeveloped as the approach road to Waterloo Bridge. Only the Savoy Chapel was left standing.

The chapel has had as colourful a history as the palace. Illegal marriages were performed here in the 1750s, which brought the building a certain notoriety. It was badly damaged by fires in 1843 and 1864, after which only the outer walls were left intact. However, the chapel was rebuilt by Robert Smirke, an architect who had carried out a great deal of restoration work on it in the 1820s.

In 1937, the building became the chapel of the Royal Victorian Order. This was founded by Queen Victoria in 1896, and enabled her to confer personal honours on people who had served her. The order was, and still is, entirely within the sovereign's personal gift and has nothing to do with ministerial advice or recommendation. Its anniversary is 20 June, the day on which Victoria became queen. When the number of members of the order became too great for the Savoy Chapel, the service was relocated to St George's Chapel, at Windsor Castle. Nevertheless, the Savoy is still the order's official chapel.

BOW STREET POLICE STATION
WC2

On 14 December 1861, Queen Victoria's world collapsed. Her 'dearest Angel', Prince Albert, died from typhoid fever in the blue bedroom at Windsor Castle. Beside herself with grief, she laid part of the blame for Albert's death on the unbecoming conduct of their eldest son, Edward, Prince of Wales, who had recently lost his virginity in an incident that was unfortunately made public. In a letter to her daughter, Vicky, the queen wrote 'Oh! that boy – much as I pity him I never can or shall look at him without a shudder as you can imagine.'

The Blue Light
It seems that, after her widowhood, Victoria experienced a similar revulsion whenever she looked at the colour blue because it reminded her

ABOVE: *Queen Victoria is reputed to be stuffy and staid, but in fact she had a lively sense of humour.*

of the heart-rending events that took place in the blue room at Windsor. This had interesting consequences for Bow Street Police Station, which was equipped with an exterior blue lamp in 1861, in common with every other police station in London. The sight of the blue light was so painful to Queen Victoria when she saw it during a visit to the nearby Opera House that she insisted it should be changed to a white one. Accordingly, Bow Street became the only police station that had a white, rather than blue, lamp.

THEATRE ROYAL, DRURY LANE
Catherine Street, WC2

Two of the many women in Charles II's life are associated with this famous theatre. The street is named for his queen, Catherine of Braganza, while the theatre itself was where one of his mistresses, Nell Gwyn, was such a popular actress. Nell knew the area around Drury Lane well as she had lodgings here; Samuel Pepys records seeing her in her doorway in 1667.

Charles II was keen to enjoy himself whenever the opportunity arose, and once he was safely back on the throne following the Restoration, he had no truck with the prevailing puritanical aversion to theatrical displays. Many theatres had been closed in London during the Civil War to stop them being used for public meetings that might provoke unrest. However, Charles was determined to reverse this trend and in 1662 he conferred a theatrical patent on two actor-managers, which licensed them to set up their own theatres. Thomas Killigrew (1613–83), who ran the King's Company, built a theatre on the site of the present playhouse. His fellow actor-manager, Sir William D'Avenant (1606–68), who ran the Duke's Company, built a theatre in Lincoln's Inn.

Players and Kings
Charles disliked the British theatrical convention of employing men to play women's roles on stage and announced that actresses should be used in future. He was not called 'the Merry Monarch' for nothing, and there was doubtless a great deal of self-interest in his new ruling. Sure enough, in 1668 he first met Nell Gwyn at the Duke's Theatre; she had made her debut at the Theatre Royal in 1665, in John Dryden's *Indian Queen*. Nell and Charles II soon became lovers and she

ABOVE: *Nell Gwyn used to appear on stage at the Theatre Royal, Drury Lane on a regular basis.*

moved to a much more respectable address in Pall Mall (see page 29), which was conveniently located close to St James's Palace, although she continued her successful theatrical career.

Charles was not the only monarch to fall in love with an actress. In 1791, the Duke of Clarence (who was later William IV) first saw the comic actress, Mrs Jordan, on stage at the Theatre Royal. They conducted a long and happy love affair, during which Mrs Jordan bore him 10 children.

Theatrical Dramas
Theatregoers to Drury Lane sometimes had very eventful experiences that bore no relation to the plays they were seeing. In 1716, a man called Freeman tried to shoot the future George II in the theatre. History repeated itself in 1800, when George III also survived an attempt on his life here. George III enjoyed visiting the Theatre Royal, as did

his son, the flamboyant Prince of Wales (later George IV). However, after they had a highly public row in the foyer, the theatre's management tactfully decided to build two royal boxes so the king and his son need not sit together in future.

The present theatre is the fifth building to stand on this spot. The original theatre was closed down in 1664–5 during the Great Plague, which was at its most virulent in the area around Drury Lane. It subsequently burnt down in 1672, and was rebuilt by Sir Christopher Wren in 1674. The third theatre was designed by Robert Adam (1728–92) in 1775 when David Garrick was the actor-manager, but was declared unsafe in 1790 and Henry Holland (1745–1806) designed its replacement. This building burnt down in 1809 and the present theatre, designed by Benjamin Dean Wyatt, was constructed.

SOMERSET HOUSE
The Strand, WC2

In 16th-century London, the Strand was a very fashionable address because it was conveniently close to the Palaces of Westminster and Whitehall. It was thronged with houses belonging to bishops and various members of the aristocracy, so it was the obvious choice for Edward Seymour (1506–52), the ambitious uncle of the young Edward VI, when he wanted to build a palace for himself in 1547. Henry VIII was dead, and Seymour was created Lord Protector and Duke of Somerset. He was looking forward to the power he would be able to exercise on behalf of his nine-year-old nephew, and decided to build a suitably grand house for himself on land he already owned between the Thames and the Strand. Various old churches and chapels already stood on the land, but Somerset soon got around such nuisances by having everything demolished. This was long before the days of preservation orders and listed buildings, of course, but nevertheless Somerset's actions provoked a furore and he enjoyed a brief spell of incarceration in the Tower of London in 1549.

Two years later, Somerset was back in the Tower, on a charge of treason, and was executed in January 1552. His glorious new palace was almost finished, having cost £10,000, and was given to the Crown. Princess Elizabeth lived in it until she became queen in 1558, when she moved to Whitehall and St James's Palaces. Somerset House was used for meetings, and provided accommodation for visiting foreign diplomats.

The building became a palace again when James I came to the English throne in 1603. His queen, Anne of Denmark, happily settled into Somerset House, which she renamed Denmark House and where she entertained lavishly. The house was remodelled for the queen, to designs by Inigo Jones, who was pressed into service again in the 1620s by Henrietta Maria, the French wife of Charles I. One of Jones's commissions was to build her a Roman Catholic chapel. This made both Henrietta Maria and her husband deeply unpopular and mistrusted in a country that was almost rabidly Protestant.

Denmark House was taken over by Parliament during the Civil War, and returned to its original name of Somerset House, becoming the quarters for General Thomas Fairfax (1612–71). It was also the repository for the royal treasures that were collected by the Parliamentarians during the war, and from

where they were sold. When Oliver Cromwell died in September 1658, his body briefly lay in state at Somerset House. He was following a royal tradition, as the bodies of Anne of Denmark and James I had also lain in state here. However, something went drastically wrong with the embalming of Cromwell's corpse, and he had to be buried in haste.

After the Restoration, Henrietta Maria moved back to Somerset House, although she was forced out by the Great Plague in 1665 and never returned. The following year, the Great Fire burnt itself out just before it reached the building. When Charles II died in 1685, his widow, Catherine of Braganza, moved to the building. While living here, she quarrelled with the Protestant monarchs, William III and Mary II, when they took over the throne in 1689. This personality clash was only resolved in 1693, when Catherine was invited to become Regent of Portugal, and left the country.

Changing Roles

Somerset House lost its popularity with widowed queen consorts after this and was used as grace-and-favour apartments. By 1775, the building was in such a state of disrepair that George III agreed for it to be demolished and for its replacement to contain purpose-built public offices, such as the Navy Board. He reserved the right for space to be created for the three societies he patronized – the Royal Academy of Arts, the Royal Society and the Society of Antiquaries. The new Strand frontage was based on the 17th-century remodelling of the riverfront façade, and the architects were William Robinson and Sir William Chambers. In 1788, John Bacon the

Elder cast the full-length bronze statue of George III, wearing a toga, which stands in the courtyard. Queen Charlotte obviously did not think much of it because she asked Bacon why it was so ugly. He replied, 'Art cannot always effect what is ever within reach of Nature, the union of beauty and majesty.'

Among the public offices to occupy Somerset House in succeeding years was the General Register of Births, Deaths and Marriages, the Principal Probate Registry and the Inland Revenue. However, some of these offices have since moved and the building is now home to three world-class collections of art: the Courtauld Institute of Art Gallery, the Gilbert Collection and the Hermitage Collection. Somerset House may no longer be a royal palace but it is still suitably regal, and full of history.

ST MARY LE STRAND
The Strand, WC2

When the Duke of Somerset decided to knock down all the buildings that stood on the site of what is now Somerset House (see page 68) in 1549, one of the churches that he demolished was the Nativity of Our Lady and the Innocents. It is claimed that one of its early rectors was Thomas Becket. Somerset's promise to rebuild the church went unfulfilled and the parishioners had to wait until the 1710s before they were given a replacement.

St Mary le Strand was designed by James Gibbs, the first of the Fifty New Churches planned for London. Built between 1714–17, it established his reputation as an architect. A 250-foot (76-metre) tall column, topped by a brass statue of Queen Anne, was going to stand next to the church, but the idea was scrapped when the queen died in August 1714 and the church was given a spire instead.

A Royal Rumour
It is claimed that Bonny Prince Charlie (1720–88), the grandson of the deposed James II, who spent his life trying to reclaim the British throne for his father, 'The Old Pretender', made a secret visit to St Mary le Strand in 1750. He allegedly renounced his Catholic faith here and was received into the Church of England. This is quite a claim, as it meant he essentially renounced the Jacobite cause for which he had fought all his life. We may never know the truth of this rumour, but it certainly adds to the atmosphere and interest of this unusual church.

OPPOSITE: *Charles II insisted that the original wooden Temple Bar should be knocked down and replaced by one made of Portland stone.*

BELOW: *When Edward VII entered the City through Temple Bar in 1903, he continued the custom of returning the Lord Mayor's sword.*

TEMPLE BAR
Fleet Street and the Strand, EC4

Until the end of the 18th century, the boundary of the City of London was marked by eight gates: Aldgate, Aldersgate, Bishopsgate, Cripplegate, Ludgate, Moorgate, Newgate and Temple Bar. They are remembered in nearby street names, but only Temple Bar has physically survived, even though it no longer stands on this original spot.

Temple Bar marks the westernmost boundary of the City of London, and from the 14th century it comprised a wooden gate topped with a prison. It was the scene of some very important occasions in the history of London, including the triumphant entry into the City of Edward, the Black Prince, on 19 September 1356 when he rode through Temple Bar accompanied by his prisoner, King John of France. In February 1503, the funeral procession of Elizabeth of York, the wife of Henry VII, stopped here on its way from the Tower of London, where she had died, to Westminster Abbey, where she was buried. In June 1533, the coronation procession of Anne Boleyn passed through the gate, which had been repaired and painted specially for the occasion. However, one of the most significant royal events took place on 24 November 1588 when Anne's daughter, Elizabeth I, rode in a chariot through Temple Bar on her way to St Paul's Cathedral (see page 44) for a service of thanksgiving for the defeat of the Spanish Armada. This is thought to be the first time that the Lord Mayor of London waited at Temple Bar so he could present the keys of the City to his sovereign. Elizabeth responded by handing him a pearl-encrusted sword. This was the start of the tradition in which the sovereign has to halt at Temple Bar and ask the Lord Mayor's permission to enter the City. He hands his Sword of State to his sovereign as a sign of his loyalty, and it is then handed back to him and carried at the head of the royal procession to show that the sovereign is in the City under the protection of the Lord Mayor.

Temple Bar survived the Great Fire of 1666, but it could not withstand Charles II's desire to rebuild it. It had become so shabby that Charles overruled the Lord Mayor's insistence that he had other things to spend the City's money on, and promised that he would make up the difference between the actual cost of the replacement and the £1,005 that the Commissioners had offered. Sir Christopher Wren was commissioned to design the replacement Temple Bar, and the rebuilding work was carried out from 1669–72. The new Temple Bar was made from Portland stone taken from the royal quarries in Dorset, and was adorned with four statues of Stuart sovereigns crafted by John Bushnell: Charles I, Charles II, James I and Anne of Denmark. Between 1684–1745, the Bar received extra decorations in the form of the severed heads and bodies of traitors, which were first boiled in salt to make them unpalatable to birds and then impaled on spikes on the Bar. Canny shopkeepers rented telescopes so passers-by could get a better look at these gruesome sights.

Temple Bar continued to mark one of the City boundaries until January 1878, when it was dismantled, stone by stone, as part of the improvement schemes that were being carried out in London. The Bar was causing too much traffic congestion, it looked old-fashioned and its maintenance was expensive, so down it came. In 1880, the brewer Sir Henry Meux bought the stones, which were lying in a builder's yard, and had them reassembled as the gateway to hisestate at Theobalds Park, Cheshunt, Hertfordshire. The original site of Temple Bar is marked by a monument to Queen Victoria.

The Return of Temple Bar
However, the story has a happy ending, because Wren's Temple Bar has returned to the City of London. Its new home is the southern gateway in Paternoster Square. It has its four Stuart statues, plus new statues of royal beasts by Tim Crawley. Stone C45 contains a time capsule of objects such

ABOVE: *Prince Henry was a keen huntsman, as shown in this engraving by Clamp, which depicts him out hunting with Lord Harrington.*

as a mobile phone, an Egyptian sixpence and photographs of Temple Bar being reassembled in Paternoster Square.

TEMPLE CHURCH
EC4

Only four round churches are still standing in Britain, one of which is Temple Church. Legend has it that it was modelled on the church of the Holy Sepulchre in Jerusalem, although some authorities say it is more likely that it was modelled on the Dome of the Rock. It was built between 1160–85, when it was consecrated by Heraclius, the Patriarch of Jerusalem, in the presence of Henry II.

Temple Church owes these very auspicious beginnings to the fact that it is the church of the Order of the Knights Templar. This order of knights was formed in 1118 in order to protect Christian pilgrims who were journeying to the Holy Land. They wore white tunics adorned with red crosses, which proclaimed that they were answerable only to the Pope. Human nature being what it is, such

absolute power was bound to be a temptation, even to an order of knights who prided themselves on their piety and sanctity. They did not baulk at inflicting punishment if they thought it necessary, as they did when they imprisoned Walter-le-Bacheler, the Grand Preceptor of Ireland. He was held in the penitential cell of Temple Church where he starved to death for disobeying the Master of the Order.

Eventually, such behaviour caught up with the knights. Their property was confiscated during the reign of Edward II and passed to the Knights Hospitaller (also known as the Order of St John of Jerusalem). These new owners leased Temple Church to the lawyers who practised in the area, an arrangement that continued until 1538 and the Dissolution of the Monasteries. However, James I reversed this measure in 1608, when he gave the freehold of Temple Church to the neighbouring lawyers, provided that they maintained the church in perpetuity. He divided it between the Inner Temple, who received the southern half of the church, and the Middle Temple, who received the northern half. Accordingly, the south window bears the crest of the Inner Temple (Pegasus, the winged horse of Greek mythology), and the north window displays the crest of the Middle Temple (the Holy Lamb and Flag). A further reminder of royal involvement is that the appointment of a new Master or chaplain is carried out by the reigning sovereign, rather than by the Bishop of London.

In common with so many City churches, Temple Church received the attentions of Sir Christopher Wren in 1682 when he was asked to improve it. Repairs were carried out in 1825 and again in 1841–42. The church was badly damaged by bombing during the Second World War, but it has since been completely restored.

PRINCE HENRY'S ROOM
Fleet Street, EC4

The house that stands here was built in Jacobean times, but its history stretches back to the 12th century when it was owned by the Order of the Knights Templar, who established themselves in the area around High Holborn in London. They also accumulated a lot of money, which inevitably led to envy and spite; Philip the Fair of France persuaded Pope Clement that the knights were guilty of many heinous crimes, including sodomy and blasphemy, and they were duly persecuted. The knights in

ABOVE: *Prince Henry's Room is named for Henry, Prince of Wales, who died in 1612. His initials and Prince of Wales feathers are painted on the ceiling.*

BELOW: *This stained-glass window from Prince Henry's Room has survived, despite the building being used as a waxworks in the 18th century.*

London were thrown into the Tower of London and their property eventually passed to the Knights Hospitallers of the Order of St John of Jerusalem. This property included what is now Prince Henry's Room, and in due course it was leased to lawyers.

In the early 17th century, part of the building was an inn called the Prince's Arms, and it kept this name after being rebuilt in 1610. The main room above the gateway was decorated with oak panelling and the three feathers of the Prince of Wales were painted on the ceiling, accompanied by the initials 'P. H.'. These represented Prince Henry, the eldest son of James I, who was invested as Prince of Wales in June 1610. Two years later, he was dead of typhoid at the age of 18.

In the 18th century, the inn became home to a waxworks and the front of the building was later boarded up. Nevertheless, the prince's upstairs room remained mercifully intact, and today it houses a permanent Samuel Pepys exhibition. His diary of the 1660s charts his career as a promising member of the Navy Office and his involvement with the Royal Family, and also records his life as a

ABOVE: *The figure of Elizabeth I above the vestry door of St Dunstan's-in-the-West is believed to be the oldest stone statue of her in existence.*

they clubbed together to buy a clock for the church. It was erected in 1671, and was the first in London to be marked with minutes as well as hours.

In 1760, almost all the city gates that had once defended the entrances to the City of London were pulled down, including the Lud Gate, which stood on what is now Ludgate Hill. This gate had been decorated with statues of Elizabeth I, King Lud (who was believed to have reigned in about 66 BC) and his two sons, and these were all preserved and moved to St Dunstan's church, where they can still be seen.

The statue of Elizabeth I was placed in a niche over the vestry door and is the oldest stone statue of her in existence. It was carved by William Kerwin and dates from 1586. As for King Lud and his two sons, they were originally placed in the parish's charnel house, but they now occupy more cheerful surroundings inside the doorway of the church.

Fleet Street was widened in 1832 and the old church had to be demolished. It was rebuilt in Gothic revival style by Richard Norman Shaw (1831–1912), and the statues of Elizabeth I, King Lud and his sons were erected in the new building. The famous clock, however, was bought by the Marquess of Hertford for his house in Regent's Park (see page 82). Happily, in 1935 Lord Rothermere, who presided over his newspaper empire in Fleet Street, bought the clock and returned it to St Dunstan's.

Londoner who observed many of the events that took place during the heady days of the Restoration.

ST DUNSTAN-IN-THE-WEST
Fleet Street, EC4

In 1666, the Great Fire of London burned itself out a short distance from this Fleet Street church. Parishioners were so grateful for their escape that

ST BRIDE'S CHURCH
Fleet Street, EC4

We owe our tradition of tiered, elaborately iced wedding cakes to the spire of St Bride's Church. In the late 18th and early 19th centuries, the aptly named Mr Rich was a pastry cook in Fleet Street, and he based the design of his wedding cakes on the spire of his nearby church. Perhaps the appropriate name of the church acted as the spur to his inspiration.

A building has stood on this site since Roman times: the remains of a Roman house are preserved in the crypt, having been discovered there by an archaeologist after the church was demolished during an air raid in 1940. W. F. Grimes, the archaeologist who worked on the project, also uncovered clear evidence of six different churches that have stood on this site since Saxon times.

It was obviously a place of importance, as King John held a parliament in the Norman church in 1210. In 1666, the 15th-century church burnt down in the Great Fire of London, and Sir Christopher Wren was commissioned to design its replacement in 1671. Wren added the famous spire in 1701–03, making it the tallest of all his steeples.

Natural Disaster

Disaster struck in 1764 when the spire was hit by lightning, which knocked off the top 8 feet (2.5 metres). It was widely agreed that the answer was to fit a lightning conductor, but there was enormous controversy over its design. George III was a keen amateur scientist so he took great interest in the vexed question of the lightning conductor, and decided that it would be best to install one with blunt ends. However, perhaps not trusting his own conclusions, he consulted several scientists, including the American polymath, Benjamin Franklin, who was the inventor of lightning conductors. Franklin favoured a conductor with pointed ends.

Despite being reduced to rubble in 1940, St Bride's was lovingly restored over 17 years, and was finally re-dedicated at a ceremony attended by Elizabeth II and the Duke of Edinburgh in 1960.

YORK WATERGATE
Watergate Walk, WC2

This elaborate gateway was designed by Inigo Jones and built by Nicholas Stone in 1626. Today it is separated from the Thames by the Embankment Gardens, but when it was built it was the direct link between the river and the garden of York House in the Strand.

York House was originally the home of the Bishops of Norwich, but after the Dissolution of the Monasteries in the 1530s Henry VIII gave the property to his brother-in-law, Charles Brandon, Duke of Suffolk. He, in turn, gave it to Mary I, who presented it to the Archbishop of York in 1556.

A Favourite of James I

In 1621, the house was acquired by George Villiers,

1st Duke of Buckingham (1592–1628), who is usually described as one of the 'favourites' of James I. This appears to be a euphemism for lover, as the two men certainly had a very close friendship, which only ended when James died in 1625. When James conferred the earldom on Buckingham in 1623, he told the assembled Lords of the Council: 'I, James, am neither God nor angel, but a man like any other... I love the Earl of Buckingham more than anyone else and more than you who are here assembled. I wish to speak in my own behalf and not to have it thought a defect, for Jesus Christ did the same, and therefore I cannot be blamed. Christ

BELOW: *George III, who was interested in such things, was involved in the design of the lightning conductor on top of St Bride's steeple.*

had his John, and I have my George.' Buckingham, who was greatly disliked by a great many people, was assassinated in 1628 and his son, also named George (1628–87), became 2nd Duke of Buckingham. He was brought up by Charles I while his mother continued to live at York House, which was popularly called Buckingham House.

Buckingham Lives On
York House was considered sufficiently royal to be confiscated during the Civil War and later taken over by General Fairfax, who was also making use of nearby Somerset House (see page 68). Rather cleverly, the young 2nd Duke of Buckingham married Fairfax's daughter, Mary, in 1657, thus ensuring that his property would be returned to him after the Restoration.

The house was demolished in the 1670s and the land built on by Nicholas Barbon, who was the main property developer of the age. Buckingham's house might have vanished but he insisted that his name should live on in the local street names, such as Villiers Street and Buckingham Street. His coat of arms can still be seen over the central archway of York Watergate, and the two lions on top, holding shields with anchors, commemorate his position of Lord High Admiral.

HOLBORN CIRCUS
EC1

One of the boundaries of the City of London slices straight through Holborn Circus, therefore dividing it between the City and Camden. The circus takes its name from the Holebourne, a tributary of the Fleet River. It is the point at which Holborn, New Fetter Lane, St Andrew Street, Holborn Viaduct, Charterhouse Street and Hatton Garden all meet.

BELOW: *Prince Albert's equestrian statue presides over Holborn Circus and commemorates his involvement in the Great Exhibition of 1851.*

Holborn Circus is also the site of a bronze equestrian statue of Prince Albert, who is wearing field-marshal's uniform and doffing his cap to the City. The statue was cast by Charles Bacon and presented to the City of London in 1874, 13 years after the prince's death, courtesy of Charles Oppenheim. Plaques at the base of the statue show the prince laying the foundation stone of the Royal Exchange in 1842, and also depict Britannia distributing awards at the 1851 Great Exhibition, over which the prince presided so successfully.

ELY PLACE
EC1

This was the site of Ely House, the London palace of the Bishops of Ely for five centuries, between the late 13th century and 1772. It was an important building; Philippa of Hainault spent Christmas 1327 here, shortly before her marriage to Edward III. She was not the only royal visitor; her son, John of Gaunt, moved here in 1381 after the Savoy Palace was destroyed during the Peasants' Revolt. It remained his residence until his death in 1399.

In 1576, Elizabeth I instructed the Bishop of Ely to lease part of the property to Sir Christopher Hatton (1540–91), who was her Lord Chancellor at the time. In the 1580s, Hatton took advantage of a vacancy at the see and built a house in the garden of the bishop's palace. This was taken over temporarily by the Parliamentarians during the Civil War, who used it as a jail for Royalist prisoners. After the Hatton line died out in 1772, the property reverted to the Crown. Ely House, which had been the home of the Bishops of Ely for so long, was by now in such a dreadful state that it was pulled down and replaced by brick-built, terraced houses. The Bishops of Ely moved to a new Ely House at 37 Dover Street.

A Saintly Relic
St Ethelreda's Church, which was built in Ely Place in about 1293 as a private chapel for the Bishop of Ely, is the only part of the original Ely House still standing. It was named for the abbess who founded the monastery at Ely in 673, and part of her hand is kept as a relic in the church. In common with parts of Westminster Abbey (see page 34), the church is one of the very few surviving buildings in London to contain Gothic architecture from the reign of Edward I in the 11th century. After the Protestant Reformation in 1538, St

ABOVE: *Ely Place was familiar to Elizabeth I, who used to visit Sir Christopher Hatton, one of her advisers, here. Hatton Garden is named after him.*

Ethelreda's became the first church in England to revert to the Roman Catholic faith. Despite being sold to Welsh Episcopalians in 1836, St Ethelreda's is now once again a Roman Catholic church.

Geographical Curiosities
Ely Place is still owned by the Crown, and is a private road whose iron gates are locked at 10 o'clock each evening. The Lord Mayor of London has no jurisdiction over the street, and even the police are not allowed to enter unless invited to do so by one of the commissioners who manage Ely Place. This is interesting enough, but even more curious is the fact that Ely Place is technically in Cambridgeshire, because it was originally part of the diocese of Ely.

There is another geographical curiosity just around the corner. The Olde Mitre Tavern stands in Ely Court, which is a narrow passage leading

from Ely Place to Hatton Garden (named after Sir Christopher Hatton and now the centre of London's diamond trade). The pub was built on part of the site of Ely House, and is therefore another little piece of London that belongs to Cambridgeshire. The preserved trunk of an old cherry tree, which once marked the boundary of the diocese of Ely, stands in the front bar. Legend has it that Elizabeth I and Sir Christopher Hatton once danced the maypole around the tree. Whether or not this is true, they had a close relationship and he was one of her most trusted advisers. When he lay dying in Ely Place at the end of 1591, Elizabeth visited him and fed him broth. Four years later, she too was dead.

GRAY'S INN
WC1

There are four Inns of Court: Gray's Inn, the Inner Temple, Lincoln's Inn and the Middle Temple. They are all places where lawyers have worked and studied for centuries, and each of them is formally referred to as an 'Honourable Society'. They are all completely independent, and are governed by the Benchers (judges from the High Court and senior barristers) who are the only people allowed to call students to the Bar.

Gray's Inn was founded in about 1370 on the site of a manor house which was the London residence of Sir Reginald le Grey, who was the Chief Justice of Chester, Constable and Sheriff of Nottingham. The Inn prospered, and in the 16th century it counted Thomas Cromwell as one of its members until he was beheaded on the orders of Henry VIII. During her reign, Elizabeth I was the Inn's Patron Lady and many of her advisers were members. It is said that the screen at the west end of the hall was made from the timbers of a Spanish galleon that was captured during the Armada, and was given to the Inn by Elizabeth herself.

GERMAN HOSPITAL
Ritson Road, E8

In the 1840s, the Prussian Ambassador to Britain, Christian, Freiherr von Bunsen, and his English wife, devised the idea of a London hospital whose

OPPOSITE: *The screen in the hall at Gray's Inn survived the Second World War because it was taken to pieces and removed for safekeeping.*

specific purpose would be to treat immigrants from what was then known as the German Federation (now Germany), and also from German-speaking countries. Official estimates at the time claimed that 30,000 Germans lived in Britain. German-speaking staff were employed, so the patients at least had the comfort of speaking to a doctor or nurse in their native language. The hospital opened in 1845 with a modest 12 beds.

In 1851, a young Englishwoman called Florence Nightingale met the Bunsens, who invited her to visit the Kaiserwerth Nursing Home on the Rhine. Her parents were outraged by the thought of the visit, but it kindled in Florence the desire to train as a nurse, and by 1854 she was heading a team of nurses in Scutari in Turkey and caring for the British soldiers who were fighting the Crimean War there.

In the meantime, back in London, the King of Prussia donated money to the German Hospital. As so often happens with such benefactors, the king was asked to play a leading role in the hospital and it was suggested that he should be named its 'Protector'. Unfortunately, this did not go down at all well with Queen Victoria. After all, she was the wife of a German prince, as well as the reigning monarch, and she made it plain that she should have been asked first.

The only answer was to compromise, and so the hospital gained four royal protectors instead of one. These were the King of Prussia, Queen Victoria, Prince Albert and Queen Adelaide who, as the widow of William IV, was Queen Dowager. Despite the nationality of the Prussian king, the hospital was deemed to have the patronage of the British Royal Family. The chairman was the 2nd Duke of Cambridge, who was a cousin of Victoria and nephew of the late George IV and William IV, so there was no doubt about the blue blood of the hospital's patrons.

During the First World War, the younger doctors returned to Germany while the senior physicians remained at the hospital. However, it was a different story during the Second World War, when all the German staff were interned as enemy aliens on the Isle of Man and their places were taken by Britons. This marked the end of the concept of a special German-speaking hospital, and another change occurred in 1948 when the hospital became part of the new National Health Service. The hospital was closed down in 1987 and is now becoming derelict.

Chapter 4

MARBLE ARCH TO HIGHGATE

Marble Arch, once the impressive entrance to Buckingham Palace until it was relocated in its present position, marks the southern boundary of this section, while Lauderdale House, where Charles II's famous mistress, Nell Gwyn, spent time, marks the northern extent. There are strong connections with the Hanoverian monarchs in this chapter, ranging from the almost absurdly flattering tribute to George I, which tops the spire of St George's Church; to the statue in Queen Square that is dedicated to Queen Caroline; and the ambitious plans for Regent's Park, which were created for the future George IV.

LEFT: *Statues on the frieze of Cumberland Terrace.*

OPPOSITE: *The steeple of St George's, Bloomsbury.*

MARBLE ARCH
W1

Most of us imagine that London landmarks have always stood in the same spot. We arrange to meet friends by them, safe in the knowledge that we will all arrive in the same place. But if a friend from the early Victorian era could somehow arrange to meet us at Marble Arch, we would find ourselves standing in different locations.

In 1827, Marble Arch was erected outside Buckingham Palace (see page 16), and it stood in the position that is now occupied by the east front of the building – which is the side that looks out on to the Queen Victoria Memorial and is best known to the public. It was designed in white Carrara marble by John Nash, who was busy remodelling Buckingham Palace at vast expense for George IV at the time, and based on the Arch of Constantine in Rome. The arch formed the main entrance to the palace, and it cost £10,000. In 1829, George IV commissioned Sir Francis Chantrey (1781–1841) to cast a bronze equestrian statue of himself, which he intended to place on top of Marble Arch. However, George died before the statue was completed and it was finally erected in Trafalgar Square.

By the time Queen Victoria and Prince Albert started their family, it was obvious that Buckingham Palace was far too small for them and would have to be extended. The most sensible solution was to move Marble Arch and turn what had been a U-shaped palace into a quadrangle by building a fourth side. In 1851, Marble Arch was relocated to its present position at the north-east corner of Hyde Park, very close to where the Tyburn gallows once stood.

Marble Arch was given its own traffic island in 1908, and now the traffic rushes around it day and night. It has three archways, but only senior members of the Royal Family – in other words, the most important ones – and the King's Troop Royal Horse Artillery are allowed to pass through them.

REGENT'S PARK
NW1

Centuries ago this area was part of the ancient Forest of Middlesex. However, by 1066 it was incorporated into the Manor of Tyburn and owned by the Abbess of Barking. This ownership continued for centuries, but it cut no ice with Henry VIII when he set about dissolving the monasteries: he simply appropriated the land for himself in 1539 and turned it into a hunting ground.

At the time, the land was known as Marylebone Park Fields, and it remained a royal chase until

OPPOSITE: *Marble Arch was completely restored in 2004 to counteract the effects of over a century of grime and traffic fumes.*

ABOVE: *Mrs Wallis Simpson had a flat in Cumberland Terrace where she used to entertain Edward VIII, whom she married in 1937.*

1646, when Charles I pledged the land to Sir George Strode and John Wandesford as security for the ammunition and arms he needed to fight the Civil War. In common with virtually every other piece of Crown property, the park was sold after Charles's execution in 1649, although it was bought back after the Restoration in 1660.

A Princely Pleasure Ground

By the 1790s, it was obvious that development of Marylebone Park would not only increase the Crown's revenue, but also improve this area of London. John Nash won the resulting competition to create the most attractive and profitable scheme with his design that involved a continuous series of terraces with two circuses and 56 villas. It is appropriate that the architect of what became Regent's Park was Nash, as he had such strong connections with the Prince Regent; it was Nash who helped the prince to convert the Royal Pavilion in Brighton from a small farmhouse into a fantasy palace.

One of the prospective projects for Regent's Park was a pleasure ground for the prince, which would be linked by Regent Street to Carlton House. George supported Nash while the project was being planned. Inevitably, it attracted plenty of criticism. Not all of Nash's plans were carried out in the end, and some of the land that had been intended for terraces of houses became the site of London Zoo (see page 84). Only eight of the villas were ever built and only two of these remain – St John's Lodge and The Holme.

Regent's Park remained private until 1845, when it was opened to the public for the first time, although initially they were allowed in for just two days each week. In the 1930s, Queen Mary's Rose Garden was developed in honour of George V's consort.

Edward and Mrs Simpson

Cumberland Terrace is the most impressive of Nash's terraces and was built from 1826–28. It was named for Ernest, Duke of Cumberland, who was a younger brother of George IV. The original plan was for this terrace to stand opposite the Petit Trianon, which was the small palace that Nash planned to create for the king, but which was never built. However, another king was a frequent visitor to Cumberland Terrace. In 1936, Edward VIII visited his American mistress, Mrs Simpson, at a flat at number 16. The story of their love affair was a hot news item in America and Europe, but it had been successfully kept from the general public in Britain until late that year, when news of the 'abdication crisis', as it was called, broke in *The Times* newspaper. Shocked and angry crowds gathered outside Mrs Simpson's flat and threw bricks through her windows; she was smuggled out of the country and travelled to France, where she waited for her divorce to be made absolute. On 11 December 1936, Edward VIII abdicated, having made an announcement to the nation on the radio that night, explaining that he was abdicating so he could marry 'the woman I love'. His position as king, and therefore head of the Church of England, prevented him marrying a divorcée. Now styled the Duke of Windsor, he left England for Austria, where he also waited for Mrs Simpson's divorce to be finalized. They were married in France in June 1937 and spent the rest of their lives in exile from Britain.

LONDON ZOO
Regent's Park, NW1

The story of London Zoo began at the Tower of London (see page 55) in 1235, when Frederick II, the Holy Roman Emperor, presented three leopards to Henry III. The choice of creatures was a

flattering acknowledgement of the three leopards that adorned the coat of arms of the House of Plantagenet, to which Henry belonged. Although Henry did not realize it at the time, this was the birth of the Royal Menagerie, which was housed at the Tower until August 1835.

The Zoological Society of London was founded in 1826, and two years later it opened London Zoo in part of Regent's Park. Initially, the zoo was not open to the public, as it had been created so that scientists could study the exotic creatures before them. More animals arrived in 1830 from the menagerie at Windsor Castle, and five years later they were joined by the inhabitants of the Tower.

London Zoo finally opened to the public in 1847 and was an instant success. Many leading architects have designed the animal houses, including Decimus Burton (1800–81), who also laid out the grounds for the zoo. Between 1962–64, the pioneering Snowdon Aviary, which was constructed from aluminium, was erected. It was designed by Princess Margaret's husband Antony Armstrong-Jones, who had been created the 1st Earl of Snowdon, in conjunction with Cedric Price and Frank Newby.

ST KATHARINE'S CHAPEL
Outer Circle, Regent's Park, NW1

St Katharine's Chapel was moved to Regent's Park from its original site at St Katharine's Dock, which was demolished to make way for new docks in the 1820s. The original chapel was founded in 1148 by Matilda (*c*. 1103–52), the wife of King Stephen, to look after 'thirteen poor persons'. Since then, it has been under the patronage of the queens of England. Although most churches were stripped of their valuables and their property sold off during the Dissolution of the Monasteries, St Katharine's evaded such a fate and was even allowed to retain Henry VIII's divorced wife, Katherine of Aragon, as its patron.

Today, the chapel is the principal Danish place of worship in London. Edward VII's widow, Queen Alexandra, granted it to her fellow Danes during the First World War. The wooden figures of Moses and St John the Baptist inside the chapel were carved by Caius Cibber and were brought to the building from a Danish church in Limehouse. Outside the chapel is a copy of the rune stone that was erected in about 980 at Jelling, Denmark by Harald Bluetooth, the nation's first Christian monarch.

OPPOSITE: *Some of the original animals in London Zoo came from the royal menageries at Windsor Castle and the Tower of London.*

ABOVE: *The statue of George I on top of the steeple of St George's Church is the only statue of the monarch to have survived in London.*

ST JOHN'S WOOD BARRACKS
Ordnance Hill, NW1

Royal birthdays and other state occasions are often celebrated by the firing of military salutes, and these are carried out by the King's Troop Royal Horse Artillery. The King's Troop also takes part in relief guard duties at Horse Guards Parade each autumn, and provides a gun carriage and team of black horses for state and military funerals. When the Troop is on parade with its guns, it takes precedence over all other regiments, and parades on the right of the line.

The King's Troop is quartered at these barracks, which were built in 1832 as the Riding Department of His Majesty's Ordnance. The King's Troop was founded in 1946 by George VI, as a saluting battery with full dress uniforms. He wanted to reintroduce a troop of Royal Horse Artillery that was mounted and dressed traditionally. When his daughter, Elizabeth II, succeeded to the throne in 1952 she requested that the name of the King's Troop remained as it was (rather than changing to Queen's Troop), in remembrance of her late father.

ST GEORGE'S CHURCH
Bloomsbury Way, WC1

'A masterpiece of absurdity' is how Horace Walpole described the statue of George I that adorns the top of the pyramid-shaped steeple of St George's Church in Bloomsbury Way. Walpole was not the only critic of this church, which was one of the eight to be built by Nicholas Hawksmoor (1661–1736) between 1716–31, as it excited a great deal of adverse comment at the time. The government were not very happy about the building either, as it went wildly over-budget and eventually cost £31,000 instead of the estimated £9,000.

The unusually shaped steeple was inspired by Pliny's description of the Mausoleum at Halicarnassus, and its base was originally decorated with images of lions and unicorns. Unfortunately, toxic fumes ate away at the carvings and their mouldering remains were removed in 1871. The statue of George I, who had succeeded to the British throne in 1714 without being able to speak a word of English, was donated by a Mr Hicks, who was brewer to the Royal Household and presumably doing his best to curry favour with the new monarch. George I was depicted in Roman

ABOVE: *This statue of Queen Charlotte had already been erected in Queen Square when George III stayed here for medical treatment in 1788.*

dress, posing as St George, the patron saint of England. The message to his subjects was clear – this man might be German, but he had every right to assume the British throne and was the country's new saviour.

QUEEN SQUARE
WC1

The queen in question is Queen Anne, who was on the throne when work began on this square in 1708. However, she had died by the time it was completed in 1720. Another queen is commemorated in the middle of the square, where a lead statue of Queen Charlotte, wife of George III, was erected in about 1775. A few years later, Charlotte became very familiar with the square because it was here in 1788 that George III stayed with his physician, Dr Francis Willis, when he became ill with what was probably porphyria, a disease of the blood that causes bizarre mental and physical symptoms. It is said that his devoted wife used to prepare his favourite food for him, while he stayed in Queen Square, in the cellars of what is now Queen Charlotte's pub.

THE BRITISH LIBRARY
Euston Road, NW1

The abiding folk memory of George III is of a mad king who lost the American colonies. Although George did have periods of insanity and Britain did lose the American War of Independence during his

reign, there is still a great deal to be said in his favour. He was a highly intelligent and cultured individual who was fascinated by science and art, and his collections of books and scientific instruments now belong to the nation. His scientific instruments are part of the collection at the Science Museum in London and his books can be found in the King's Library, at the British Library.

The British Library only came into existence in 1973, when the British Museum Library, the National Central Library and the National Lending Library for Science and Technology were brought together. The British National Bibliography and the Office for Scientific and Technical Information both joined the library in 1974, followed by the India Office Library and Records in 1982 and the British Institute of Recorded Sound in 1983. As its name suggests, the British Library is the national library of the United Kingdom, and contains some of the most important books in the world.

The King's Library in housed in a tall glass tower, called the King's Library Tower, within the British Library. It contains books printed mostly in Britain, Europe and North America between the 13th and 19th centuries. George III started the collection because the previous royal library (known as the Old Royal Library and now also part of the British Library) had been given to the new British Museum by George II in 1757. There were books in the different royal residences but no properly organized library existed, so George III set about creating one. His agents travelled around Europe,

BELOW: *The King's Library was started by George III, who was a very intelligent and cultured man. He also collected scientific instruments.*

buying everything from individual books to complete libraries. By the time of his death in 1820, George III's library contained about 65,000 printed books as well as pamphlets and manuscripts.

The King's Library had a fairly peripatetic existence in its early days, as it was first housed in the Old Palace at Kew, before being moved to the Queen's House, which was later rebuilt as Buckingham Palace (see page 16). When George IV succeeded to the throne in 1820 and decided to extend the Queen's House, the books were moved once again and eventually the library was offered to the nation in 1823. After spending several years at Kensington Palace (see page 99), the library was given a permanent home in the King's Library Gallery within the British Museum. However, a small part of the collection was damaged during a German bombing raid in September 1940, and the books were sent for safe-keeping to the Bodleian Library, Oxford, for the rest of the war. In 1998, the King's Library was moved to its present home in the new British Library building.

Among the treasures of the collection is the prayer book of Lady Jane Grey, which she carried to the scaffold when she was executed for treason in 1554. She was a pawn in her father-in-law's plan to control the English throne and was briefly proclaimed queen of England before being imprisoned and beheaded in the Tower of London (see page 55).

Despite the rarity of many of the books in the King's Library, it continues to be a working library. Many of the books are displayed behind special glass panels so they can be easily viewed.

LAUDERDALE HOUSE
Waterlow Park, N6

In Elizabethan times, this was the home of Richard Martin, who was Lord Mayor of London twice and also the Master of the Royal Mint. When the house came into the hands of the 2nd Earl of Lauderdale in the 1640s it was pulled down and rebuilt. However, the English Civil War was raging at the time, and when the newly named Lauderdale House was finished it was taken over by John Ireton, who had family connections with Oliver Cromwell (Ireton's brother, Henry, was Cromwell's son-in-law). The 2nd Earl of Lauderdale regained the house after the Restoration in 1660 and later loaned it to Charles II so his mistress, Nell Gwyn, could spend the summer here.

Nell Gwyn was one of Charles II's favourite mistresses and, in common with several of her rivals, bore him children. This is somewhat ironic considering that all his children by his wife, Catherine of Braganza, were stillborn. Nell Gwyn was naturally very keen to ensure that her children by Charles should have secure futures, and she found ingenious means by which to do it. It is said that while staying at Lauderdale House she threatened to drop her baby son, Charles, out of a window unless his father immediately made provision for his future. Thinking quickly, Charles II shouted out 'Save the Earl of Burford!'

Chapter 5

WEST LONDON

West London is one of the most obviously royal parts of London. Today, it includes some of the most expensive real estate in Britain, such as Eaton Square and Knightsbridge, but only three centuries ago it was quiet, pretty countryside. This was what attracted William and Mary to the area, who were looking for a home away from the bustle and smells of central London. They chose to live in what is now Kensington Palace, and immediately put this part of West London on the world stage.

LEFT: *Since its restoration in the 1990s, the many splendours and ornate design of the Albert Memorial can once again be fully appreciated.*

OPPOSITE: *The bronze statue of William III outside the South Front of Kensington Palace was presented to Edward VII by Kaiser Wilhelm II.*

HYDE PARK
W1, W2, SW7

It is often remarked that London's parks are its lungs, in which case Hyde Park contributes more than all the other green spaces to the purification of the city's air because it is the largest of all the royal parks. It appears to be even larger than it really is because its western boundary merges into Kensington Gardens, making it difficult to establish where one park ends and the other begins. In fact, the demarcation line runs from Victoria Gate on the Bayswater Road, down Buck Hill Walk, across the Serpentine Bridge and south to Alexandra Gate, which sits at the point where Kensington Gore meets Kensington Road. This ceremonial gate is a remnant of Prince Albert's Great Exhibition of 1851. The park's three remaining boundaries are obvious: it is bordered to the north by the Bayswater Road, to the east by Park Lane and to the south by the Brompton Road, Knightsbridge and Kensington Road.

As with so many great London landmarks, we have Henry VIII to thank for Hyde Park. He first spotted the potential of this stretch of land in 1536, during the Dissolution of the Monasteries, when he took it from the monks of Westminster Abbey and turned it into another of his many hunting grounds. Elizabeth I also enjoyed hunting here. The public was given limited access to the park for the first time in the 17th century, during the reign of James I, but it was his son, Charles I, who opened it fully to the public.

Parliament sold off the park in 1652, but it became a royal possession once again after 1660 when Charles II returned from exile in Europe to claim the throne. He had a brick wall constructed to surround the park, and, presumably, to keep out the riff-raff. However, during the Great Plague of 1665, which killed so many of his subjects, Charles allowed military encampments to set up within the park.

A Royal Water Feature

In the 18th century, gardening became one of the great royal pleasures. Queen Caroline, wife of George II, was particularly interested in landscape gardening. In the late 1720s, she decided that

OPPOSITE: *After the Serpentine lake was created in Hyde Park in the 1730s, the Royal Family enjoyed sailing on it in their two yachts.*

Hyde Park needed a lake. One of London's many rivers, the Westbourne, was dammed to create this water feature, which took three years to complete and was named the Serpentine. Whenever the lake's water level drops too low, it is topped up by a pump, which is located on Duke Island in nearby St James's Park (see page 21).

Fireworks, Riots and a Crystal Palace

Hyde Park has been the scene of some memorable occasions. In 1821, the celebrations for George IV's coronation included firework displays and hot-air balloons. That same summer, there were riots when the funeral cortège of George's estranged wife, Queen Caroline, tried to pass through Cumberland Gate (named for George's brother, the Duke of Cumberland). The fighting was so intense that soldiers had to intervene. In 1851, the Great Exhibition was held in the park. Various sites were proposed for the event, including Regent's Park. Hyde Park was eventually chosen, despite scare stories in *The Times* announcing that 'Kensington and Belgravia would be uninhabitable and the Season would be ruined'. The Great Exhibition was organized by Prince Albert, and aimed at demonstrating Britain's supremacy as a world power. The event was a wild success. It was housed within the massive Crystal Palace that was designed by Joseph Paxton (1801–65), ran between May and October 1851, and was visited by over 6 million people. Queen Victoria attended the event frequently, visiting roughly every other day during its first three months. In 1852, the Crystal Palace was dismantled and moved to a new site at Sydenham in south London, although the ceremonial entrance gate remained in Hyde Park. More recent royal events here have included the Queen's Silver Jubilee Exhibition, which took place in 1977, and a royal fireworks party, which was held in July 1981 to celebrate the marriage of Prince Charles and Lady Diana Spencer.

One of the more curious facts about Hyde Park concerns the Broad Walk, which runs to the west of Park Lane. In 1954, the elm trees that grew either side of it were cleared to create a wide path that could double as an emergency air strip if the Royal Family needed to leave London in a hurry. So far, they have not made use of it.

HYDE PARK CORNER
SW1

This was originally the site of a toll gate for people entering London. However, in the 18th century, it was decided that the area should be tidied up and made to look more imposing. Constitution Arch, also known as the Wellington Arch, which stands in the centre of Hyde Park Corner, was commissioned by George IV who wanted to create a grand entrance to Buckingham Palace. He gave the commission to Decimus Burton, who completed it in 1825. The arch was erected in 1828, close to Apsley House, the home of the Duke of Wellington (1762–1852), but it was moved to its present position in 1882 in order to line up with the top of Constitution Hill. It was originally adorned with a massive statue of the 'Iron Duke', as Wellington was popularly called, on horseback, but this was so large that it provoked an equally big controversy. When the arch was relocated in 1882, the statue was tactfully removed. Its replacement, a bronze group called *Quadriga* by Adrian Jones, was presented by Lord Michelham in 1912 in memory of his friend, Edward VII.

To the north of Hyde Park Corner is the Hyde Park Screen, which was also designed by Decimus Burton in the 1820s. It was intended to be an impressive link between Hyde Park and Buckingham Palace, and it incorporates a frieze based on the Elgin Marbles.

ABOVE: *The Queen Elizabeth Gates were erected in honour of the late Queen Mother. The details on the gates reflect some of her many interests.*

Just around the corner, at the start of Park Lane, are the Queen Elizabeth Gates which were designed by Guiseppe Lund with sculptures by David Wynne. The gates were unveiled in 1993 by Queen Elizabeth II in the presence of her mother, Queen Elizabeth the Queen Mother, whose life they celebrate.

A more recent royal memorial was opened on 6 July 2004, when Queen Elizabeth, accompanied by other members of the Royal Family and representatives of the Spencer family, opened a memorial fountain dedicated to the late Diana, Princess of Wales.

MANDARIN ORIENTAL HOTEL, HYDE PARK
Knightsbridge, SW1

This building began life in 1882 as a select apartment block, but it reopened as the Hyde Park Hotel in 1908. The original main entrance, which faced Hyde Park, was for the exclusive use of royalty; the Knightsbridge entrance was for the *hoi polloi*.

Throughout the 20th century, the Hyde Park Hotel was popular with members of the Royal Family. During the First World War, Queen Mary visited the soldiers who stayed here when on leave. Her son, Edward VIII, enjoyed chatting to members of staff while he was out of the public gaze. When they were young girls, the Princesses Elizabeth and Margaret had dancing lessons here from Madame Vacani. In recent years, the hotel has undergone a change of name and is now known as Mandarin Oriental Hyde Park.

ROTTEN ROW
SW7

One of Hyde Park's main features is Rotten Row, which runs in a straight line near its southern boundary. It was originally called '*route du roi*', because it was the path that William III used to take when he walked between his home in Kensington Palace and St James's Palace. By all accounts, William seems to have been someone who enjoyed ill-health and who was always waiting for the next disaster to befall him. Walking the *route du roi* in the dark made him extremely nervous. He was justified in fearing for his personal safety because Hyde Park was a notorious haunt of highwaymen during the late 17th century. As a result, William took the precautionary measure of having 300 oil lamps suspended from the trees along the route to light his way in the dark. Rotten Row therefore became the first English road to be illuminated at night.

ABOVE: *Rotten Row was originally William III's route between Kensington and St James's Palaces.*

EATON SQUARE
SW1

This very expensive and exclusive London square was built by Thomas Cubitt (1788–1861) from 1826–55. He cannily recognized the potential of the area around Buckingham Palace after serious work began on converting it into a lavish palace for George IV. The square was named after Eaton Hall in Cheshire, which is the country seat of the Grosvenor family who owned much of the land in this part of London. In common with so many other select London residential areas of the time, Eaton Square was built over a sewer, in an age when typhoid fever was extremely prevalent. The disease affected everyone from the poorest members of society to the Royal Family: Queen Victoria suffered from it in 1836, the year before she came to the throne and, in 1861, typhoid killed her husband, Prince Albert.

Nevertheless, its proximity to a noxious sewer did not deter members of society from moving into Eaton Square and its neighbouring streets. One of the square's earliest residents, at number 13, was George Fitzclarence, Earl of Munster (1794–1842). He was the eldest illegitimate son of William IV and Mrs Jordan, and married Mary, the illegitimate daughter of George Wyndham, 3rd Earl of Egremont.

Eaton Terrace, just around the corner, was a favourite haunt of George Fitzclarence's cousin, Edward, Prince of Wales (later Edward VII). He took his mistresses to the apartments at number 55, where the concierge, Mrs Rosa Lewis, was his friend. She later became the celebrated owner of the Cavendish Hotel in Jermyn Street. However, Edward's visits to Eaton Terrace ceased after he came to the throne in 1901, as he was required to lead a more discreet lifestyle. His years as Prince of Wales had certainly been notable for their scandals.

ABOVE: *The statue of Charles II, in full Roman dress, was not erected in the South Court of the Royal Hospital until 1692, long after his death.*

THE ROYAL HOSPITAL
Royal Hospital Road, SW3

This is popularly known as the Chelsea Hospital and its residents are called Chelsea Pensioners. They are veteran soldiers, and about 450 of them live here at any one time, divided into six companies.

The Royal Hospital has stood on this Chelsea site for over 400 years. It was established as a direct result of the English Civil War. Until then, Britain did not have a standing army, so there was no need to provide a home for its old soldiers. However, all that changed after the Restoration. In 1681, Sir

Stephen Fox (1627–1716), the first Paymaster General, and Nell Gwyn, Charles II's mistress, suggested that there should be an English equivalent of the Hôtel des Invalides in Paris. Sir Christopher Wren was appointed architect and Charles laid the foundation stone in 1682. The first soldiers took up residence in 1689, by which time Charles was dead, his brother James II had made a tactical exit to France, and William and Mary had arrived from Holland to take the throne.

May Celebrations

The hospital's central courtyard contains a bronze statue of Charles II, which was designed by Grinling Gibbons (1648–1720). Each year, on 29 May, Oak Apple Day, which is Charles II's birthday and the anniversary of his formal restoration to the throne in 1660, Chelsea Pensioners don tricorn hats, carry sprigs of oak leaves and adorn the statue with more oak leaves.

May is an important month in the calendar of the Royal Hospital because this is when the Chelsea Flower Show is held in part of the grounds. It has been held here since 1913, and is staged by the Royal Horticultural Society, one of whose former presidents was Prince Albert. There is a special preview on the Monday evening before the show opens the next day, which is always attended by several keenly horticultural members of the Royal Family. In 2003, Prince Charles helped to design one of the gardens.

ABOVE: *One of the most famous department stores in the world, Harrods is illuminated at night by thousands of electric lights.*

Close to the hospital is Royal Avenue. When William and Mary moved into Nottingham House, which became Kensington Palace (see page 99) in 1689, they required a road that connected their new home with the Royal Hospital. Work started from the Chelsea end, but it was never extended past the King's Road (see below).

KING'S ROAD
SW3, SW6, SW10

Note the name. This is the King's Road and, until 1830, that is precisely what it was: a private road for the reigning sovereign and the privileged few who were considered important enough to be allowed to use it.

King's Road was built after Charles II's succession to the throne in 1660, as a swift route for the royal party between Whitehall Palace and Hampton Court (see page 121). London streets in the 17th century were narrow, uneven and congested with horses, carts, people, carriages and the smelly detritus that accompanied them, so it made sense to create a private short cut for royalty. Other well-connected people were allowed to use the road, provided that they produced a special copper pass, which bore the stamp of the monarch's monogram on one side and the words 'The King's Private Roads' on the other. George III later used the road whenever he travelled to his palace at Kew.

HARRODS
Brompton Road, SW7

You might expect to find a royal shrine in a cathedral or the chapel of a royal palace, but it is another matter to stumble across one when shopping in one of the world's most famous department stores. Nevertheless, shoppers in Harrods can combine some satisfying retail therapy with a thought-provoking visit to a shrine to the late Diana, Princess of Wales and her companion, Dodi Al Fayed.

Located next to the Central Egyptian Escalator, the shrine was erected by Dodi's father, Mohamed Al Fayed, who owns Harrods. On display is a wine glass that the couple used on their final evening in Paris, as well as the ring that Dodi bought for Diana on the day before their deaths. Debate still rages about whether this was an engagement ring, and also about Diana's thoughts on the matter.

Until December 2000, Harrods was the proud owner of four royal warrants: those of the Queen,

Queen Elizabeth the Queen Mother, the Duke of Edinburgh and the Prince of Wales. A royal warrant is rather like a royal stamp of approval, as it proclaims that a particular business is patronized by a senior member of the Royal Family. The business has to apply for the royal warrant every five years and it is renewed if relations between the business in question and the royal person are still harmonious. Harrods had proudly displayed its four royal warrants for many years, not only outside the shop, but also on all its merchandise, packaging and stationery. However, in January 2000, the Duke of Edinburgh announced that he would be withdrawing his royal warrant from Harrods at the end of that year because he no longer shopped there. Although this was a perfectly reasonable explanation, it was widely believed that the duke's decision did not concern his shopping habits so much as the accusations that Mohamed Al Fayed had made about his alleged involvement in arranging the car crash that killed Diana and Dodi.

The other three royal warrants were still operational, but Al Fayed announced that he would not apply for their renewal when the time came and, in December 2000, he had them all removed from the front of the building. They also vanished from everything else connected with Harrods.

THE VICTORIA AND ALBERT MUSEUM
Cromwell Road, SW1

When a building has a name like this, there is no need to ask which members of the Royal Family are associated with it. This world-class museum of the decorative arts was one of the projects that Prince Albert championed following the Great Exhibition of 1851. It was originally an amalgam of the Museum of Manufactures and the School of Design, which were both housed in rather makeshift quarters on the site now occupied by the Victoria and Albert Museum, or V & A as it is popularly known.

By the 1880s, it was clear that the museum's collections had swelled to such an extent that there was no longer space for them all. They needed a proper, purpose-built home, and in 1890 a competition was launched to find the best design. Aston Webb, the architect who later designed the Queen Victoria Memorial (see page 22) was the winner, but it was not until 1899 that Victoria laid the foundation stone. By now she was 90: it turned out to be the last major official engagement

ABOVE: *Although the wedding of Queen Victoria and Prince Albert in 1840 was a dynastic alliance, it was also the culmination of their love affair.*

that she ever attended. At the ceremony, she announced that the building should henceforth be called the Victoria and Albert Museum.

The V & A was finally completed in 1909, at a cost of over £600,000, and was opened by Edward VII. As if anyone should be in any doubt about the museum's royal connections, the top of the central tower is shaped like a crown, and statues of Victoria and Albert and Edward VII and Queen Alexandra flank the main entrance. The museum contains many treasures, including some with royal connections. The Raphael Cartoons, which have their own gallery, were bought for the Royal Collection in 1623 by the future Charles I and were first lent to the museum by Queen Victoria; they are now on loan from Queen Elizabeth II. You can also see tapestries stitched by Mary, Queen of Scots, the wedding suit of James II, the Dark Jewel given to Elizabeth I by Sir Francis Drake and Holbein's miniature of Anne of Cleves.

THE SCIENCE MUSEUM
Exhibition Road, SW7

The Science Museum is part of a complex of museums and universities around a small area in South Kensington. Like its near neighbour, the Victoria and Albert Museum (see page 95), it was founded after the success of the Great Exhibition in 1851 and enjoyed the support of Prince Albert.

The origins of the Science Museum lie in a collection known as the Museum of Manufactures, which opened on the first floor of Marlborough House (see page 28) in 1852, before being moved to South Kensington and temporarily housed in a building nicknamed the 'Brompton Boilers'. It was part of the South Kensington Museum, which also housed what became the separate collection of decorative art that is now the Victoria and Albert Museum. The Science Museum, as it was eventually known, outgrew the space allotted to it. The East Block, which is the main building in Exhibition Road, was opened by George V in 1928.

One of the most important collections in the museum is the King George III Collection. George III was fascinated by science and amassed an important collection of scientific apparatus made for him by George Adams, as well as mathematical models and surveying instruments. Many of the items from the collection are on show, including George's Grand Orrery.

BELOW: *The frieze around the exterior wall of the Royal Albert Hall depicts 'The Triumph of Arts and Sciences'. The hall itself is oval.*

THE ROYAL ALBERT HALL
Kensington Gore, SW7

This part of London is so well-stocked with memorials to Prince Albert, consort of Queen Victoria, that you might be forgiven for thinking it should be renamed 'Albertovia' or something equally appropriate. The Albert Memorial is nearby, but even its gilded magnificence pales by comparison with the vast red-brick dome of the Royal Albert Hall.

After the financial success of the Great Exhibition of 1851, Prince Albert suggested that the profits should be used to create a complex of museums, schools, colleges and a hall in South Kensington. The Kensington Gore Estate was duly bought the following year. However, the project to create a big concert hall failed to get off the ground and was still in limbo when Albert died unexpectedly of typhoid fever in 1861. Money was collected from the public to pay for the Albert Memorial and a concert hall, but it was not nearly enough to pay for both ventures. In the end, the money for the Hall of Arts and Sciences, as the Royal Albert Hall was originally called, was raised by selling 999-year leases on its seats. The building was designed by Sir George Gilbert Scott (1811–78), who also designed the Albert Memorial, and Queen Victoria laid the foundation stone in 1867. At the end of the ceremony, she dropped the bombshell that the hall should be given the prefix of 'Royal Albert'. The hall was opened four years later by Victoria's son, the Prince of Wales, because his mother's emotions were so overwhelming that they prevented her being present at the opening ceremony.

The Royal Albert Hall became a popular venue for concerts and balls, despite its appalling acoustics, which were not improved until 1968. In 1911, over 80 royal guests attended the Shakespeare Ball here, as they were all in London for the coronation of George V, which took place a few days later. In 1937, George VI's Coronation Ball was held here, and the tradition was continued for his daughter, Elizabeth II, in 1953.

A further memorial to Prince Albert can be found by the South Steps outside the Royal Albert Hall. This memorial was originally intended to commemorate the Great Exhibition. It was created by Joseph Durham in 1863, and was first erected in the grounds of the Royal Horticultural Society, moving to its present position in 1899.

THE ALBERT MEMORIAL
Kensington Gardens, SW7

Opinion remains divided on the merits of the Albert Memorial. To some, it is a typically overblown example of the sort of mawkish, sentimental monument that Queen Victoria was so fond of erecting in memory of her dead consort, Prince Albert. To others, it is a wonderful example of High Victoriana in all its pomposity, especially since it was restored in the late 1990s to all its original gilded glory.

At first sight, the memorial is certainly startling, especially when the sunlight catches its shiny surface. During the First World War, the gilding was removed for fear that it would act as a landmark for German Zeppelins hoping to bomb Kensington Palace. It stands 175 feet (53 metres) high, with seven tiers of statuary and enormous marble groups, which represent Asia, Europe, Africa and America. A white marble frieze runs around the base of the memorial, decorated with 169 life-size figures of celebrated musicians, poets, painters, architects and sculptors. The Gothic canopy is inlaid with semi-precious stones, including jasper, onyx and carnelian, and topped with an orb and cross. In the middle of all this is a statue of Prince Albert himself, seated and wearing the collar of a Knight of the Garter, with the garter on his left leg. The catalogue of the Great Exhibition of 1851, which he championed so vigorously, lies open on his knees.

The monument cost £120,000, and some of the money was raised through subscriptions to the Royal Society of Arts, of which the prince had been president. It took 12 years to build, and was designed by George Gilbert Scott, who was knighted by his grateful queen after she first saw it in 1872. The bronze statue of Prince Albert was cast by John Foley and erected in 1876. To his grieving widow, the prince's memorial doubtless

ABOVE: *Queen Victoria herself chose the design of the Albert Memorial, and closely monitored every stage of its planning and construction.*

fell far short of reality, but at least she heartily approved of Scott's intention to create a shrine to Prince Albert's sainted memory.

KENSINGTON GARDENS
W8

In marked contrast to what often feels like the dusty sprawl of Hyde Park, Kensington Gardens seems much more intimate. Perhaps it is the

ABOVE: *Kensington Gardens evolved in tandem with Kensington Palace, as successive monarchs acquired stretches of the surrounding land.*

knowledge that one of the great royal palaces lies within the park and that Kensington Gardens once formed its private garden.

The history of Kensington Gardens is closely linked with that of Kensington Palace (see page 99), which stands near the western boundary of the gardens. The first royal occupants of the new palace were William and Mary, who arrived in 1689. Mary had a strong artistic and decorative eye, and she commissioned Henry Wise and George London to landscape the gardens in the formal Dutch style, with box hedging and rows of tulips. This was not a hit with the next royal incumbent, Queen Anne, who had all the plants dug up and replaced with a more relaxed, English style of planting.

However, Anne did approve of the formal wilderness, north of the palace, which William had commissioned from London and Wise. Work was interrupted by William's death, but Anne had barely succeeded to the throne before she told the gardeners to continue. The Orangery, which is still in use, was designed by Nicholas Hawksmoor and modified by Sir John Vanbrugh. It was built in 1704–05 near the entrance to the wilderness, and provided an outdoor room in summer and shelter for tender plants in winter. Anne was also responsible for the stone summerhouse, which originally stood at the south end of Dial Walk, but now lies at the north end of the fountains, near Lancaster Gate.

In 1725–26, George I put his stamp on the gardens by installing some exotic animals, including wild cats, in the paddock. However, they did not stay here very long, and were relocated to the menagerie at the Tower of London (see page 55) in 1727 after the death of the king. This move may have been the suggestion of Queen Caroline, wife of George II, who was a keen gardener and had her own ideas about the design of Kensington Gardens. She may have been less than enthusiastic at the idea of encountering tigers and civet cats whenever she took a stroll around the gardens of her new palace. Both the Broad Walk and the Round Pond, which was originally intended to be rectangular, were created during this time. The Queen's Temple, which still stands, was a revolving summerhouse designed by William Kent and built in 1734–35.

A Park for the 'Respectably Dressed'

George II followed the tradition of other royal parks by opening the gardens to the public, although he restricted the opening hours to each Saturday when the court was at Richmond. He also stipulated that only 'respectably dressed people' could be admitted, and that soldiers, sailors and liveried servants should be denied entrance. It was not until the 1830s, and the reign of William IV, that the public was allowed into the gardens at any time of the year. However, by this time the palace was no longer the home of the reigning sovereign, as Buckingham Palace (see page 16) now fulfilled that function.

National Grief
In September 1997, the area of Kensington Gardens just outside the gates of Kensington Palace became the focus of an extraordinary out-pouring of national mourning after the sudden death of Diana, Princess of Wales. The gardens near the Crowther Gates were covered in a blanket of tens of thousands of flowers and toys, all laid there in the memory of the princess, who had lived at Kensington Palace until her death.

KENSINGTON PALACE
W8

If William III had not suffered from asthma, it is doubtful that Kensington Palace would ever have been built. When he and his wife, Mary, came to the throne in 1689, following the hasty departure of the previous incumbent, James II, the official London palace was Whitehall. This was very near the Thames, making it convenient for visiting Parliament when it was sitting, but highly inconvenient for William whose chronic bronchial problems were exacerbated by the damp, riverside air. There was also the ticklish question of smell, as at the time the Thames was basically an open sewer into which London's waste was eventually discharged (having polluted the city's other rivers, which flowed into the Thames, first). The royal nose would have been mightily offended by the rank stench that floated towards Whitehall on a warm day, and so William and Mary made it their first priority to find somewhere else to live.

They settled on Nottingham House, which was a Jacobean mansion in what was then the village of Kensington. It was too small, of course, so they commissioned Sir Christopher Wren to rebuild it. William and Mary must have been exacting clients for Wren, because they wanted everything done in a great hurry and Mary frequently visited the house

'to hasten the workmen'. In November 1689, her chivvying ended in disaster when some of the new buildings fell down and killed several workmen. Despite this, work continued and the Royal Family was in residence by Christmas, despite the fact that the house was far from finished.

Mary's instincts in telling the workmen to hurry were prophetic: she died of smallpox in the palace in 1694. This was a highly dangerous and disfiguring disease, and Mary insisted that everyone who had not had it should leave the palace before they caught it. William remained at the palace until his death in 1702, from complications that set in after he broke his collarbone in a fall from his horse at Hampton Court (see page 121).

Queen Anne, who suffered from ill health all her life and had to be carried to her coronation because of her degenerative arthritis, enjoyed living at Kensington Palace. Her husband, the slow-witted Prince George of Denmark, was asthmatic and the 3rd Earl of Sheffield remarked that it was only the prince's heavy breathing that told his courtiers he was still alive. Anne died here in 1714, and the crown passed to her third cousin, George I.

Hanover Comes to Kensington
George, who left his divorced wife Sophia behind in Germany when he travelled to Britain to take the throne, liked Kensington Palace because it reminded him of his family home, Schloss Herrenhausen, in Hanover. His new palace needed a great deal of renovation and three new state rooms were added: the Privy Chamber, the Cupola Room and the Withdrawing Room. William Kent, who at the time was barely known, made his name by painting all the ceilings and creating the *trompe l'œil* on the King's Grand Staircase.

When George II and Queen Caroline moved into the palace on their accession in 1727, they were the last reigning monarchs to live here. Their turbulent family life was dramatically played out in

ABOVE: *George II enjoyed the gardens of Kensington Palace as well as the building itself. He was the last reigning monarch to live here.*

ABOVE: *The South Front of Kensington Palace was added in 1695. William III's wind-vane stands on top of the façade between the Portland stone vases.*

the palace; they had an almost pathological hatred of their eldest son, Frederick, Prince of Wales, which they made no secret of. Their enmity towards him was so pronounced that Caroline once said 'Our first-born is the greatest ass, the greatest liar, the greatest *canaille* and the greatest beast in the world and we heartily wish he was out of it.'

When not shouting at the Prince of Wales, the king and queen kept themselves busy by decorating the palace in the latest fashion. They spent a lot of money on furniture and fabrics, but carried out little building work. Caroline died in 1737, after which many rooms in the palace were shut up and no longer used. When George died in his lavatory at the palace in 1760, it was the end of an era. George III had no desire to live here and it was neglected. It quickly became dilapidated, so it cost a small fortune to renovate it when some of the apartments were earmarked for various members of the Royal Family at the end of the 18th century. The Duke of Wellington was so incensed at the amount of money it cost to house the Royal Family that he described them as 'the damndest millstone about the necks of any government that can be imagined'.

ABOVE: *The South Front of Kensington Palace was added in 1695. William III's wind-vane stands on top of the façade between the Portland stone vases.*

One of these 'millstones' was Edward, Duke of Kent, fourth son of George III. Like his elder brother, who later became George IV, the duke had a talent for spending money that he did not own, and even had to leave the country at one point to escape his creditors. He returned in 1818 after the sudden death of Princess Charlotte, the heir to the throne, the year before. A new heir was needed, and quickly, so the duke married Victoria, Dowager Princess of Leiningen and on 24 May 1819 their daughter, Princess Victoria, was born in Kensington Palace. Her christening took place that June in the Cupola Room. The duke died the following January and his widow brought up Victoria in the palace, having altered the State Apartments, against the wishes of William IV, so they could live in them.

The Victorian Age Begins
On the momentous morning of 20 June 1837, Princess Victoria was woken with the news that her

uncle, William IV, had died and she was now queen. She and her mother moved into Buckingham Palace the following month, but Kensington Palace was still lived in by other members of the Royal Family, including the Duke and Duchess of Teck and their daughter, Princess Mary, who was born here. As a young woman, she became engaged first to Prince Eddy, Duke of Clarence, but he died in 1892, giving Mary a lucky escape from marriage to a man who was never far away from scandal. The following year, she married his brother, George, Duke of York (later George V). In the early 1930s, Queen Mary, as she was by then, was instrumental in renovating Queen Victoria's Apartments. By this time, the State Apartments were open to the public, having first been opened on Queen Victoria's 80th birthday on 24 May 1899.

Kensington Palace Today

Today, Kensington Palace is still home to some members of the Royal Family. Princess Margaret lived here until her death in 2002. When Prince Charles married Lady Diana Spencer in July 1981, the palace became their official London residence. After they separated, Princess Diana continued to live at the palace and Prince Charles moved to St James's Palace. 'KP', as it is popularly known by its inhabitants, has to combine three main functions: it is a private residence; a major tourist attraction; and a working palace. It is also a fascinating building, full of architectural and historical interest.

ST MARY ABBOTS CHURCH
Kensington Church Street, W8

Several churches have stood on this site, after the first one was built in the 12th century. Its replacement was built in 1370, but this was pulled down and replaced in the 1690s to create a suitably impressive church for William and Mary, who had moved into nearby Nottingham House, which was without a private chapel. William contributed towards the building costs and donated the pulpit and reading desk. However, this church was demolished in 1772 and rebuilt, before George Gilbert Scott was commissioned to build the present church in 1869–72.

In 1821, Kensington Church Street lay on the route of Queen Caroline's funeral cortège. Her funeral should have been a solemn occasion but the public treated it as a chance to vent their fury at what they saw as George IV's appalling treatment of her. He had prevented her taking any part at all in his coronation only a few weeks before, and had also instigated a trial at the House of Lords to investigate her supposedly adulterous behaviour – which many thought was a classic case of the pot calling the kettle black. When the funeral cortège entered Kensington Church Street it was greeted by a mob that threw obstacles in the way of the horses. The funeral procession had no option but to double back and go past Hyde Park (see page 90), where further disruptions took place.

ABOVE: *Kensington Palace contains the Royal Ceremonial Dress Collection. This is a waxwork of Queen Mary, who was born in the palace in 1867.*

Chapter 6

SOUTH-EAST LONDON

This section of London is dominated by Greenwich, which, thanks to its proximity to the Thames, has played a crucial role in royal life since the first palace was built here in the 15th century. There are still many reminders of Greenwich's importance, from the Queen's House to the Old Royal Observatory. Nearby is Blackheath, whose position on the London–Dover road made it the scene of some dramatic events in the history of British kings and queens.

LEFT: *Eltham Palace was a popular royal residence until it was eclipsed by Greenwich Palace late in the reign of Henry VIII.*

OPPOSITE: *The time-ball on the roof of the Old Royal Observatory allowed ships in the Thames to check the accuracy of their chronometers.*

THE PRINCE CONSORT'S MODEL LODGE
Kennington Park, SE11

If you are a prince consort you can pull strings that are not available to other people. This is why Prince Albert was able to persuade the organizers of the Great Exhibition of 1851 to allocate the adjoining site in Kensington Gardens (see page 97) to the Society for Improving the Conditions of the Labouring Classes.

At the time, the conditions of the working classes in Victorian Britain were a national scandal – they were damp, insanitary, crowded and often inhumane. By contrast, the Model Lodge that was displayed at the Great Exhibition was designed by Henry Roberts to provide decent habitation, including what was then the luxury of an indoor lavatory. The design was subsequently used for housing in various parts of London.

After the exhibition closed, the Model Lodge was moved to its present position in Kennington Park, where it became the home of two park attendants in addition to being a museum. An inscription below the balcony states 'Model houses for families erected by HRH Prince Albert'.

LAMBETH PALACE
Lambeth Palace Road, SE1

This has been the official residence of the Archbishops of Canterbury since 1207, when it was called Lambeth House and was the home of Stephen Langton (*c.* 1157–1228). The oldest surviving part of the palace is the crypt, which dates from the 13th century; the chapel was built soon afterwards. The palace has been extended and modernized on various occasions over the centuries, including in 1553 when Queen Mary ordered that it should be refurbished for Cardinal Pole (1500–58); strangely enough, they died within hours of each other in 1558.

Drama was played out in the Guard Room in 1534 when Thomas More was interrogated by Thomas Cromwell after he refused to sanction Henry VIII's decision to appoint himself head of the Church. When the English Civil War broke out in 1642, Lambeth House, as it was still called, was taken over for public service and became a prison during the Commonwealth, with the chapel being used for dances. Naturally, the building was greatly damaged, and after the Restoration in 1660 the Great Hall was rebuilt under Archbishop Juxon (1582–1663).

Today, the Great Hall is a library that contains the leather gloves that Charles I is alleged to have handed to Archbishop Juxon on the scaffold, shortly before his execution in January 1649. The library also houses the medical reports of George III, whose life was blighted so severely by what is believed to have been porphyria.

GREENWICH PARK
SE10

The oldest of the enclosed royal parks, Greenwich Park has stunning views across the Thames. It was created in 1433 when Humphrey, Duke of Gloucester (1390–1447), the brother of Henry V, walled in the land around his home, which later became Greenwich Palace.

The park and the palace became favourites of that keen hunter of deer and women, Henry VIII; he managed to satisfy both appetites at Greenwich. May Day was a time of celebration, when Henry

LEFT: *The Prince Consort's Model Lodge is a testament to his social conscience about the living conditions of the working classes.*

ABOVE: *Lambeth House has long been the official residence of the Archbishops of Canterbury, but it was used as a prison during the Civil War.*

BELOW: *In 1572, Elizabeth I presided over a mock battle in Greenwich Park after the Duke of Norfolk's plot against her was quelled.*

held regular sporting events in the park. On May Day 1515, Henry and his first wife, Katherine of Aragon, held a sumptuous picnic in the park for the Venetian ambassador. Every comfort had been taken care of, even to the extent of placing caged songbirds in the trees above the guests' heads. By contrast, the May Day revels of 1536 were an occasion for tension and fear for Henry's second wife, Anne Boleyn: it was the last time she ever saw her husband, as she was arrested for treason and sent to the Tower of London (see page 55) the following day. Soon after the accession of Anne's daughter, Elizabeth I, in 1558, the City of London held a magnificent party for her in Greenwich Park.

When Charles II returned from exile to take the throne in 1660, he commissioned the French landscape gardener André Le Nôtre to redesign the park. Many elms and Spanish chestnuts were planted during the same decade. In 1675, the Royal Observatory (see page 107) was built on the site of the Duke of Gloucester's home.

Greenwich Park was first opened to the public in the 18th century, but people really began to flock here a century later, as the railway line between Greenwich and London Bridge opened in 1838, and a steamboat service between Greenwich and Central London began in 1854. By this time, the park was still owned by the Crown, although the palace had long since been deserted by its royal residents.

The Sailor King

In 1935, a statue of William IV, which had originally been erected in King William Street in the City of London, was moved to King William Walk in Greenwich. The statue was created by Samuel Nixon in Foggit Tor granite. It is an appropriate site for the man who had joined the Navy as a midshipman at the age of 13 and became known as the 'Sailor King', as the National Maritime Museum is situated nearby.

ABOVE: *William IV, whose statue stands in King William Walk, had long experience of life in the Royal Navy before he became king in 1830.*

OPPOSITE: *The time-ball on the roof of the Old Royal Observatory is a reminder of the important scientific work that has been carried out here.*

THE OLD ROYAL NAVAL COLLEGE
Greenwich, SE10

This complex of four buildings is all that remains of the medieval Greenwich Palace, which was a favourite residence of the Tudor sovereigns. The original riverside palace was built by Humphrey, Duke of Gloucester (1390–1447), who called it Bella Court. As its name suggests, it was considered to be one of the most beautiful houses in medieval England. Humphrey was a cultured man and was the first private individual in England to create an important library, which he bequeathed to Oxford University, where it became the centre of what is now the Bodleian Library.

Humphrey was also a generous man. In 1445, he lent Bella Court to his nephew and niece, Henry VI (1422–61, 1470–71) and Margaret of Anjou (1429–82), for their honeymoon. Such kindness counted for nothing two years later when Humphrey fell out with Margaret, and she had him imprisoned and – it is said – murdered. Henry and Margaret moved into Bella Court with unseemly haste a few days after Humphrey's death. Henry VII had the palace rebuilt in 1490, renaming it Placentia, 'the pleasant place'. It was here that his son, the future Henry VIII, was born in June 1491 and married his first wife, Katherine of Aragon, in June 1509 and his fourth wife, Anne of Cleves, in January 1540.

Henry VIII loved Greenwich Palace. It was here that his daughters, Mary and Elizabeth, were born in February 1516 and September 1533 respectively. Henry's sole legitimate son, Edward VI, died at the palace in July 1553. He would have been appalled at the fate of the palace during the Civil War, when it was first put up for sale and then, when there were no takers, turned into a biscuit factory. After the Restoration in 1660, Charles II decided to rebuild the palace and call it the King's House, but only one block was completed when the project had to be suspended in 1669 for lack of money.

The Birth of the Naval Hospital

When William and Mary succeeded to the throne in 1689, they had little interest in the King's House because they feared that its proximity to the dank and smelly Thames would exacerbate William's asthma. Mary wanted the house to be demolished, which it was in 1694, and rebuilt as a naval hospital. However, the original design would have blocked the view of the river from the Queen's House (see page 108), and vice versa, so the buildings were split into their current arrangement. Mary died before the work began, and the foundation stone for the new hospital was laid by Sir Christopher Wren, as architect, and John Evelyn (1620–1706), as treasurer, in June 1696. Work continued for the next 50 years, under a variety of different architects, including Sir John Vanbrugh, Nicholas Hawksmoor and James 'Athenian' Stuart. There are four blocks: King Charles's building, Queen Anne's building, King William's building and Queen Mary's building. Together, the buildings are considered to be the finest example of Baroque architecture in England. The only trace of Greenwich Palace still standing is the under-croft of Queen Anne's building.

The naval hospital was not a complete success and it was closed in 1869 amid accusations of ill-treat-ment and corruption. In 1873, the Royal Naval College moved here from Portsmouth, where it stayed until 1998. The buildings have since been taken over by the University of Greenwich and Trinity College of Music. Nevertheless, the grounds of the Old Royal Naval College, plus the Painted Hall and the chapel, are open to the public.

The Elephant and the Maypole

Nearby is Five Foot Walk, which is where George I landed on 18 September 1714, having succeeded to the British throne after the death of Queen Anne the previous month. He left his divorced wife in Hanover and brought with him two of his three mistresses, who must have been a comical sight as one was extremely fat and the other immensely thin. Sophia von Kilmansegg, who was later created Countess of Darlington, was known as 'the Elephant' at court because of her size. Horace Walpole gave a vivid description of her: 'the fierce black eyes, large and rolling between two lofty arched eyebrows, two acres of cheeks spread with crimson, an ocean of neck that overflowed & was not distinguished from the lower part of her body, and no part restrained by stays.' Her fellow mistress was Ermengarda Melusina von Schulenburg, later created Duchess of Kendal, who was popularly

called 'the Maypole' because she was so tall and thin. George had two daughters by her. Walpole had a strong opinion of her, too, describing her as 'a very tall, ill-favoured old Lady'.

THE OLD ROYAL OBSERVATORY
Greenwich Park, SE10

In March 1675, Charles II appointed John Flamsteed (1646–1719) the first Astronomer Royal. The next step was to build a suitable observatory in which Flamsteed could work.

Various sites were proposed, but Sir Christopher Wren swayed the argument in favour of Greenwich Hill. On 22 June that year Charles duly founded the observatory. Flamsteed's first brief was 'to apply himself with the most exact care and diligence to the rectifying of the tables of the motions of the heavens, and the places of the fixed stars, so as to find out the so much-desired longitude of places for the perfecting of the art of navigation'.

Charles promised to buy some of the astronomical instruments that would be required, but, as happened so often with him, he failed to provide the money, so Flamsteed had to purchase the equipment himself. The astronomer carried out most of his work in Sextant House, which can still be visited today.

In 1833, a time-ball – the first of its kind in the world – was erected on top of the Octagon Room. This signalled the time to ships travelling along the Thames. The time-ball still drops at precisely 1 o'clock each afternoon. Another important event took place in 1884, when it was formally announced that the Prime Meridian should run through royal Greenwich, giving it the longitude of 00° 00' 00". A brass strip on the ground marks this point.

London's appalling light pollution led to the transfer of the Royal Observatory from Greenwich to Herstmonceux, Sussex in the late 1950s, and from here it later moved to Cambridge. The observatory buildings at Greenwich were taken over by the National Maritime Museum, which displays many important historical astronomical instruments.

THE QUEEN'S HOUSE
Greenwich, SE10

In 1605, James I gave Greenwich Park (see page 104) and Greenwich Palace to his wife, Anne of Denmark. This was probably intended as some consolation for their rather unsatisfactory marriage: modern historians consider that James was probably homosexual, and his close relationships with Robert Carr, later Earl of Somerset, and George Villiers, later the Duke of Buckingham, seem to attest to this. In 1616, Inigo Jones was commissioned to build a new house for Anne in the grounds of Greenwich Park. However, work on the Queen's House did not progress very far before she died in 1619.

'The House of Delights'
In 1629, Anne's son, Charles I, gave the unfinished building to his queen, Henrietta Maria, commissioning Jones to complete the project. The building was completed in 1640, much to the joy of Henrietta Maria who called it 'the house of delights'. Unfortunately, the Civil War intervened and in 1642 Henrietta Maria left England for Holland, where she hoped to raise the money to buy arms and equip Royalist soldiers. In November that same year, Parliamentary forces searched the Queen's House for weapons; they found no trace, but they confiscated the building. Many of the treasures within the house were sold, but the house was retained and used for the lying-in-state of Commonwealth generals.

Greenwich Palace was badly damaged during the Commonwealth and in 1662 Charles II decided that it would have to be pulled down and rebuilt. At the same time, he commissioned John Webb to enlarge the Queen's House, as this was to serve as a royal residence while Greenwich Palace was being reconstructed. After the Restoration, Henrietta Maria briefly returned to her old house in 1662, before moving to Somerset House (see page 68). In 1670, the Queen's House was given to Charles's wife, Catherine of Braganza, and in 1685 it became the property of James II's second wife, Mary of Modena (1658–1718), but she had little use for it. It was the same story when William and Mary came to the throne in 1689, so in 1690, it was given to the Earl of Dorset, who was the first Ranger of Greenwich Park.

In 1694, work began to transform Greenwich Palace into a hospital. This new development placed the Queen's House at its central point, so there was still uninterrupted space between the residence and the Thames. The house became part of the hospital, but its upkeep was very expensive.

When George I landed at Greenwich on 18 September 1714, he held his first official reception in the Queen's House the following day. In 1805, his great-grandson, George III, appointed Princess Caroline of Brunswick, the estranged wife of the Prince of Wales, as Ranger of Greenwich Park. The Queen's House became her official residence, but in 1806 she leased it to the Royal Naval Asylum, a school for sailors' orphans, in an attempt to clear her debts. The school moved out in 1933 and in 1937 the Queen's House was opened as part of the National Maritime Museum. It has since been restored to its 17th-century appearance and is open to the public.

BLACKHEATH
SE10

Blackheath was once notorious for the numerous highwaymen that made this stretch of the journey between Dover and London so dangerous. The road did not become safe until the surrounding area was developed into a residential suburb in the 18th century, and when the railway arrived in 1849 another wave of building commenced. Blackheath's position on the London–Dover road means that it has been the scene of some very important events in British history. In 1415, Henry V rode through Blackheath on his return to England after his victory at the Battle of Agincourt. During the Cornish Rebellion of 1497, Henry VII defeated Michael Joseph and his fellow Cornish rebels in a battle on the heath. In January 1540, Henry VIII travelled to Blackheath to meet his new queen, Anne of Cleves. The meeting was a diplomatic success, but it was a romantic and dynastic failure. The couple were married three days after meeting, but divorced six months after that.

There was more spectacle and rejoicing on Blackheath when Charles II rode here on horseback to meet General Monck and his army on his restoration to the throne in May 1660.

Cloth of gold might not have adorned the scene, as it did for Henry and Anne, but the route was thronged with happy people who were longing to see their new ruler, delighted that the monarchy, and their old way of life, had returned.

The Ranger's House
Nearby is the Ranger's House, which was built between 1699–1700. It was the home of the Duchess of Brunswick, mother of Caroline, Princess of Wales, between 1807–14. The duchess wanted to be near her daughter, whose marriage to the Prince of Wales (later George IV) was by then over in all but name and who attracted scandal the way jam attracts flies. In 1815, the house became the official

BELOW: *The Queen's House has been restored to its 17th-century appearance so its architectural and decorative splendours can be fully appreciated.*

residence of the Ranger of Greenwich Park. Princess Sophia Matilda, the great-granddaughter of George II, lived here until her death in November 1844. In 1902, the Ranger's House became a cafeteria after it was sold to London County Council, but it has now been restored and converted into an art gallery, housing the Suffolk Collection of 17th-century Jacobean and Stuart portraits.

ROTHERHITHE
SE16

This old area of London dockland was originally called Redriffe. Samuel Pepys knew it by this name, but it had already been thriving for centuries before. In fact, it is believed that early in the 11th century, King Canute (1016–35) laid siege to London from here when he dug a trench that stretched from Rotherhithe to Vauxhall.

When the Domesday survey was carried out in 1086, Rotherhithe was part of the royal manor of

ABOVE: *The Mayflower pub in Rotherhithe is named after the ship that moored nearby before taking the Pilgrim Fathers to America in 1620.*

OPPOSITE: *Eltham Palace is a fascinating blend of ancient and modern, with a 1930s house built onto the side of the Elizabethan great hall.*

Bermondsey. In the 14th century, a royal fleet was fitted out at Rotherhithe on the orders of the Black Prince and John of Gaunt, both sons of Edward III. In 1413, Henry IV (1399–1413) retreated to Rotherhithe, suffering from what was thought to be leprosy and which apparently killed him, although an examination of his corpse in 1832 refuted this.

The Cuckolding King
Downriver of Rotherhithe is Cuckold's Point, a site that was once marked by a pair of horns (the symbol of a cuckold) mounted on top of a pole. This was the starting point of the annual Horn Fair that proceeded to Charlton. According to legend, Cuckold's Point gets its name because King John seduced the wife of a local miller and, in order to pacify him, gave him this stretch of land.

The remains of a moated manor house, which was built for Edward III in 1361 and excavated in the 1980s, can be found at Bermondsey Wall East and Cathay Street.

ELTHAM PALACE
SE9

There has been a royal connection with Eltham since at least 1086, when the Domesday Book recorded that the manor of Eltham was owned by Odo, Bishop of Bayeux and half-brother of William the Conqueror. In 1305, the manor house was rebuilt by Anthony Bek, Bishop of Durham, and given to Edward, Prince of Wales, who later reigned as Edward II. He presented it to his wife, Isabella of France (*c.* 1294–1358), after their marriage in 1308 and she was a frequent visitor; the couple's second son, John, was born here in 1316.

Succeeding kings played their part in the history of Eltham Palace. Richard II instigated some improvements to the palace, which were carried out under the supervision of Geoffrey Chaucer. The great hall, which is the most impressive part of the palace to have survived, was built in the 1470s, during the reign of Edward IV (1461–70, 1471–83). It still has the third largest hammerbeam roof in the country.

Medieval Modernism
The role of Eltham Palace as a favoured royal residence effectively came to an end during the reign of Henry VIII. He spent a great deal of time here as a boy, but in later life he much preferred nearby Greenwich Palace. His daughter, Elizabeth I, also

favoured Greenwich over Eltham. The palace was sold off during the Interregnum, which followed the execution of Charles I, and was partially pulled down by its new owner. The great hall was used as a barn for the next two centuries and the rest of the palace was left in ruins.

This once great palace would probably have rotted away had it not been for Stephen and Virginia Courtauld, who bought it in 1931 and began a lengthy restoration programme. Although it seems an extraordinary act in today's architectural climate of preservation orders and listed buildings, the Courtaulds built a highly contemporary, Art Deco house right next to the great hall so they could move seamlessly between the 15th and 20th centuries. They also landscaped the gardens, which included converting what was once the moat into a sunken garden. This extraordinary combination of medieval and modern was requisitioned by the army during the Second World War, but Eltham Palace is now owned by English Heritage and is open to the public.

THE ROYAL NAVAL DOCKYARDS AND ARSENAL
Woolwich, SE18

Woolwich is the home of one of Henry VIII's greatest achievements – the Royal Dockyard, which he established in 1512. It was an inspired move as it was much closer to London, where cannons were manufactured, than the original dockyard in Portsmouth; it was also conveniently close to Greenwich Palace, so Henry could keep a watchful eye on progress. The first ship to be built at Woolwich was the Great Harry, which was the largest ship in the world when she was launched in 1514 and the flagship of the English navy. Another dockyard was created upriver at Deptford in 1513, and it was here that Elizabeth I knighted Francis Drake after he had successfully circumnavigated the world in April 1581.

The Royal Arsenal also dates from Tudor times, but was originally situated in Moorfields in the City of London, and was known as the Warren. However, the arsenal was relocated to Woolwich after a tragic explosion in 1713 that killed 17 people. It was renamed the Royal Arsenal by George III in 1805, at which point it was heavily engaged in helping to create the ammunition for the Napoleonic Wars.

The dockyards at Woolwich and Deptford closed in 1869, as they had failed to keep up with the latest technological advances and were also struggling to cope with the heavy amounts of silt that the Thames was depositing in their harbours. Although both areas were developed for housing, many of the old dockyard buildings have been kept and are still visible today.

The Royal Arsenal also eventually moved out of Woolwich in 1969, and in recent years the area has been developed into shops, offices and museums.

Chapter 7

SOUTH–WEST LONDON

Each area of London has its own distinctive character and this area of London offers leafy royal parks and breathtaking vistas of the Thames as it winds its sinuous way towards the heart of the city. One of the most notable places in this section is the Royal Botanic Gardens, which began life as the garden of Kew Palace. Another is the magnificent, sprawling palace of Hampton Court, which was appropriated by Henry VIII from his Lord Chancellor as a penance and became one of the most impressive buildings in the world.

LEFT: *The Chinese Pagoda in the Royal Botanic Gardens was erected in the 18th century.*

OPPOSITE: *The moat bridge in front of the central gateway of Hampton Court Palace is lined with stone carvings of the King's Beasts.*

ROYAL BOTANIC GARDENS
Kew, Surrey

In the 18th century, this area formed the private gardens of Frederick, Prince of Wales, which are today known as the Royal Botanic Gardens. At the time, Kew was a place of political intrigue, having grown in importance during the previous two centuries because of its close proximity to nearby Richmond Palace. Whenever the court sailed downstream to Richmond for the summer, away from the threat of plague and the stench of the Thames at Whitehall, all the courtiers followed and many of them settled in Kew.

Frederick was a very keen gardener, having already created a landscaped garden at Carlton House in London, and he set about doing the same thing at Kew. Frederick was greatly aided in this task

ABOVE: *Many royal gardeners, most notably Princess Augusta, have enjoyed working on what are now known as the Royal Botanic Gardens.*

by John Stuart, the 3rd Earl of Bute (1713–92), who was briefly Prime Minister in 1762–63. He helped the prince to design the gardens and to collect many of the plants and trees that became the basis of the world-renowned collection of the Royal Botanic Gardens. On 31 March 1751, Frederick died from complications that set in after he caught a chill while gardening in the rain. His widow, Augusta, continued to live at the White House, which was one of the residences within the gardens. She also continued to work on the gardens with Bute, prompting some ribald gossip about the nature of their relationship. Their work at Kew was helped by William Chambers (1726–96), who was the architectural tutor to Augusta's son, George, Prince of Wales, and a noted expert on Chinese culture. He undoubtedly had a very strong influence on the plethora of Chinese-inspired buildings that sprang up in the grounds of Kew – the Chinese Pagoda is one of the few extant buildings from that time. Other buildings at Kew were inspired by foreign cultures as well, including the classical Temple of Bellona, which was named for the Roman goddess of war, and an Islamic mosque that no longer exists. In 1761, Chambers also designed the building that is now known as the Orangery for Augusta; at the time, such structures were becoming meeting place in which to play cards, drink tea and entertain one's friends.

By the end of her life, Augusta was only an occasional visitor to Kew, but she had helped to landscape over 100 acres (40.5 hectares), which contained more than 2,700 species of plants. It was a colossal achievement and is commemorated in the Princess of Wales Conservatory at the Royal Botanic Gardens, which was opened by Diana, another Princess of Wales, in 1987.

KEW PALACE
Kew, Surrey

Kew Palace is set like a miniature jewel within the vast expanse of the Royal Botanic Gardens (see above). The palace began life as the Dutch House and was built in red brick around 1613 by a Dutch merchant called Samuel Fortrey. It was one of the first examples in Britain of a brickwork known as 'Flemish bond', in which the bricks are laid with their sides and ends alternating. The rounded gables gave the house its distinctive Dutch appearance. Fortrey lived here with his wife, Catherine, and their initials can still be seen above the entrance.

The Dutch House was leased in 1728 by Queen Caroline, who intended to use it as a royal annexe whenever she and her husband, George II, were staying at nearby Richmond Lodge. The Dutch House became a nursery for the royal children, and George III spent a lot of time here as a boy. Caroline also leased several other buildings and plots of land, including the White House which stood nearby. In 1731, the White House became the home of Frederick, Prince of Wales. He was the despised eldest son of George II and Queen Caroline, so even the thought of his nearby presence must have been vexatious to them. However, he and his wife, Augusta, were rare visitors to Kew until the death of Caroline in 1737. After that, they lived at Kew, devoting much of their time to creating what are now the Royal Botanic Gardens.

In 1772, the White House was taken over by Frederick and Augusta's son, George III, and his young family. George, Prince of Wales (who became the Prince Regent in 1811 and George IV in 1820) and his younger brother, Frederick, lodged nearby at Kew Palace. The freehold of the property was given to their mother, Queen Charlotte, in 1781.

Although the life of what we now know as the Royal Botanic Gardens continued to develop, and still flourishes today, Kew Palace enjoyed only a brief flowering. By 1818, it was the end of an era. On 13 July 1818, William, Duke of Clarence and his younger brother, Edward, Duke of Kent, were both married in a joint ceremony at Kew Palace. A crisis had been triggered the previous year by the death of Princess Charlotte, the daughter of the Prince Regent, in childbirth. The Royal Family needed more heirs, and in effect the two brothers embarked on a race to see who could produce a child first. It was a sad irony that the Duke of Clarence had fathered numerous healthy, illegitimate children, most notably by his

ABOVE: *Kew Palace was a private royal residence for less than 100 years between the reigns of George II and George IV.*

long-time and devoted mistress, Mrs Jordan, but none of his legitimate children survived early infancy. The Duke of Kent and his wife, Victoria, were more fortunate and produced a daughter who grew up to become Queen Victoria.

On 17 November 1818, Queen Charlotte died at Kew Palace, and it was closed. The Royal Botanic Gardens acquired the palace, with Queen Victoria's permission, in 1896, and it was opened to the public two years later. The present garden

ABOVE: *The Queen's Cottage in the Royal Botanic Gardens was built in the 1770s for Queen Charlotte to use as a summerhouse.*

behind the palace, known as the Queen's Garden, was opened by Elizabeth II in 1969 and contains the classical busts of figures that originally stood in the innovative gardens of Carlton House, created in the 18th century by the Queen's ancestor, Prince Frederick.

SYON HOUSE
Brentford, Middlesex

Syon Park has been the London residence of the Percys, the Dukes of Northumberland, for over 400 years. Contained within more than 200 acres (80 hectares) of parkland, the present house was built by Robert Adam in the 1760s and stands on the site of an abbey dedicated to St Bridget and named after Mount Zion, which was founded by Henry V in 1415. However, in common with so many similar English properties, Henry VIII acquired the abbey in 1539 during his Dissolution of the Monasteries. The Father Confessor of the nuns had already been executed in 1535 on Henry's orders for refusing to accept the king as the head of the new church, and his body was exhibited on the gateway to the abbey to set an example to everyone else. In November 1541, Henry's fifth wife, Katherine Howard (*c.* 1525–42), was accused of high treason and sent to Syon Abbey, to await the outcome of the

investigations that were conducted into the behaviour of her alleged lovers; she was beheaded at the Tower of London (see page 55) in 1542. There is a rather macabre ending to Henry's association with the area. When he died in 1547, grossly overweight and suffering from complications caused by a chronic leg ulcer, his body was carried from Whitehall Palace to Windsor Castle. En route it rested overnight in the ruined chapel at Syon Abbey. During the night, his lead coffin burst open and the following morning dogs were found lapping up his blood on the floor of the church.

Between 1548–51, Edward Seymour, 1st Duke of Somerset, who was the Lord Protector of Henry's heir, Edward VI, built a house on the site. This passed to John Dudley, Duke of Northumberland (*c.* 1502–53) – no relation of the current family – after Somerset's execution in 1552. He had aspirations to become the power behind the throne by making his daughter-in-law, Lady Jane Grey, queen. She was offered the crown in the Long Gallery at Syon and accepted it reluctantly: she was right to be wary, as she only reigned for nine days before being overthrown by Mary I and sent to the Tower, where she was executed. In 1594, Syon Park passed into the hands of Henry Percy, 9th Earl of Northumberland (1564–1632), and it has remained in the family ever since.

There seems to be a path that leads from Syon House to the Tower, and the 9th Earl trod it in 1605 through no fault of his own. His cousin, Thomas Percy (1560–1605), dined with the earl at Syon and then travelled up to London where he joined forces with his fellow Roman Catholic conspirators, among whom was Guy Fawkes, and attempted to blow up Parliament the following day. Thomas Percy was shot while trying to escape and his hapless cousin, the 9th Earl, was considered to be guilty by association, and was detained in the Tower for 15 years on the orders of James I.

The 10th Earl, Algernon (1602–68), had happier royal connections, being the governor to Charles I's younger son, James, Duke of York between 1646–49. The duke and his siblings lived at Syon House in 1646 and Charles was able to visit them here from time to time. The 3rd Duchess of Northumberland continued this educational tradition when she was official governess to the young Princess Victoria in 1831–37, at which point her 18-year-old charge became Queen Victoria.

ABOVE: *Drama was played out at Syon House in 1553 when its owner, the Duke of Northumberland, tried to put Lady Jane Grey on the throne.*

RICHMOND PALACE
Richmond-upon-Thames, Surrey

Once one of the great medieval royal palaces, all that remains now of Richmond Palace is the old gatehouse on the south side of Richmond Green, and a trio of houses in Old Palace Yard, which date from the reign of the Tudors. Old engravings of the palace show a sprawling building of several stories, with many turrets and chimneys, standing on the banks of the Thames. There is a model of the palace at the nearby Richmond Museum.

Richmond Palace started life as a manor house in the 12th century. At the time, this area was known as Shene and was a popular hunting ground. Henry I acquired the manor house in 1125, although Edward III was the first king to spend a lot of time here and he also lavished plenty of money on the place. Edward died here in June 1377, dependent on his ambitious mistress, Alice Perrers, who had persuaded the servants to wrench the rings from his fingers. Edward's grandson, Richard II, inherited the throne and, with it, Shene Palace. It was his favourite summer residence, where he and his first wife, Anne of Bohemia (1366–94), entertained with lavish generosity. However, medieval summers always brought the plague, and the disease killed Anne in June 1394. Richard experienced such intense grief that he ordered the destruction of Shene Palace. Nevertheless, some parts of it were left standing and were used by Henry V as the basis for a major programme of restoration.

Tudors and Stuarts

Shene was a particular favourite of Henry VII, and he had the palace rebuilt in grand style after it burnt down in 1499. It was at this point that its name was changed to Richmond, after Henry's earldom in Richmond, Yorkshire. Two of Henry VIII's children by Katherine of Aragon were born and died here, and in 1554 his daughter, Mary I, spent part of her honeymoon here after her marriage to Philip of Spain. In March 1603, the dynasty of the Tudors ended when Elizabeth I died in Richmond Palace.

RICHMOND PARK
Richmond-upon-Thames, Surrey

There have been deer in Richmond Park for hundreds of years, and it has been a favourite royal hunting ground since the 13th century, when it was still known as Shene Chase. If you can manage to screen out the noise and sight of passing cars and aircraft, it is comparatively easy to picture the park as it might have been when Edward I knew it, thanks to its mixture of ancient broadleaf trees, wild deer and stretches of bracken.

In 1637, Charles I acted against the wishes of local residents and his own advisers by enclosing the park with a high wall that still stands today. At least he allowed pedestrians the right to walk through the park, which was a privilege that Princess Amelia, one of George II's daughters, rescinded after she became the Ranger of the park in 1747. Only her closest friends were allowed access to the park, a stricture that aroused so much local antagonism that she was forced to resign her position. Ladderstile Gate, which is situated near Kingston Hill, commemorates this victory of the people over the Crown.

Richmond's Lodges
Princess Amelia lived at White Lodge, to the east of the park, while she was Ranger. This Palladian villa was also a favourite residence of her mother, Queen Caroline, and had been commissioned by George II. In the 1890s, White Lodge was the home of the Duke and Duchess of Teck, whose daughter, Mary, married the future George V in 1893. It was here, in June 1894, that Mary gave birth to her eldest son, who later became Edward VIII. In the 1920s, White Lodge was the home of the Duke and Duchess of York who, much to their horror, became King George VI and Queen Elizabeth after the abdication of Edward VIII in 1936. In the

ABOVE: *Only the gateway and three houses remain of the once great Richmond Palace. It was originally called Shene Palace.*

Richmond Palace passed to the Stuart kings and was therefore an inevitable casualty of the Civil War of the 1640s. Most of the palace was destroyed after the execution of Charles I in 1649, and although Charles II later had it restored for his mother, she found it too bleak. The palace gradually fell down, until more memories than stones remained.

mid-1950s White Lodge was taken over by the Lower School of the Royal Ballet School, and they are still here.

Pembroke Lodge, to the west of the park near Petersham, also has an interesting history. It was originally the home of the park's molecatcher, but in 1780 George II gave the house to his friend, the Countess of Pembroke, after whom it became known. It later became the home of Elizabeth, Countess of Errol, who was an illegitimate daughter of William IV and his long-standing mistress, Mrs Jordan.

ORLEANS HOUSE GALLERY
Twickenham, Middlesex

A villa originally stood on this site, built in 1710 for James Johnston, who was the Joint Secretary of State for Scotland under William III. A few years later Johnston commissioned James Gibbs to build a Baroque garden pavilion known as the Octagon. It was intended to amuse Caroline, Princess of Wales, who was married to the future George II, during a visit to the house.

Between 1815–17, the house was the home of the exiled Duc d'Orléans (1775–1850), who later returned to his native France and reigned as Louis Philippe Égalité, King of the French, from

1830–48. Two years after his death, his widow, Maria Amalia, bought Orleans House and it stayed in the family until 1877. Most of the house was demolished in the 1920s, although Gibbs's Octagon survived and is now part of the Orleans House Gallery, which stands on this site.

Marble Hill
Nearby, in Chiswick Mall, is another house with connections to Caroline. The Palladian Marble Hill House was built in 1729 for Henrietta Howard (1681–1767), later the Countess of Suffolk, with money given to her by George II. She was the king's mistress for over 20 years and, as if that were not galling enough for his wife, Caroline, she was also one of her ladies-in-waiting. In 1795, the house was taken by another royal mistress, Mrs Fitzherbert. In 1785, she had entered into an illegal marriage with the future George IV.

After being allowed to fall into a state of disrepair for a number of years, Marble Hill House has now been restored by English Heritage and one of its highlights is Lady Suffolk's Bedchamber.

ABOVE: *Bushy Park was first enclosed by Henry VIII so he could use the land for hunting deer, which was one of his favourite sports.*

BELOW: *Henry VIII was a very able and active sportsman until his increasing girth and the pain from his leg ulcer started to slow him down.*

BUSHY PARK
Hampton, Middlesex

This is the second largest of the royal parks and it spreads north of its nearest green neighbour, Hampton Court Park. These two parks have always been connected historically because originally they both belonged to the Knights Hospitallers of St John. In 1514, the land was acquired by Cardinal Thomas Wolsey, who at the time was busy establishing a little empire for himself which centred around Hampton Court Palace (see page 121). Irreconcilable differences between Wolsey and Henry VIII led to the cardinal's downfall, and in 1528 he gave all the land, along with his palace, to the king. Henry had the parks enclosed so he could use them for his favourite sport of hunting. Of course, Henry enjoyed the pursuit of many different things, including women, but in this case the quarry was deer.

Bushy Park was now a royal possession and so it passed from sovereign to sovereign. Over the centuries, three of those monarchs made an important contribution to the park. The first king to make his mark was Charles I, who decided to create the artificial stretch of water, Longford River, in Bushy Park. Designed by Nicholas Lane, the river was created entirely by hand, a task that took nine months from 1638–39.

The other main feature of the park was created on the orders of William and Mary, who were both keen gardeners. They ordered Sir Christopher Wren to design an avenue, which would provide a formal approach to Hampton Court Palace, running from Teddington Gate on the northern boundary of Bushy Park. This long, straight avenue is lined on each side with a single row of horse chestnut trees and four rows of lime trees, and circles a small lake. Wren placed the bronze fountain, topped with a statue of Diana, the huntress, in the centre of the lake in 1713.

During the First World War, parts of Bushy Park were dug up and used to grow crops as part of the war effort. George V gave permission for Upper Lodge, one of the buildings in the park, to become a home for convalescent Canadian soldiers who were often visited by Queen Mary. Areas of the park were once again put under the plough during the Second World War, and in 1942 it became the site of a large US base called Camp Griffiss. The park was the headquarters of various Allied departments, and was where Operation Overlord, which led to the D-Day landings of June 1944, was planned.

THE CORONATION STONE
Kingston-upon-Thames, Surrey

Is this the coronation stone upon which seven Saxon kings were crowned? Yes, according to the names carved on the plinth at its base. This lump of sandstone, fenced in by *faux* Saxon railings, graces Kingston's High Street outside the Guildhall. Kingston is the oldest of only three Royal Boroughs in England, having gained its charter from King John in 1200, so it definitely has important royal connections. The name of the town suggests that the provenance of the stone may be correct, for surely 'Kingston' could be a corruption of 'King's Stone'? In fact, 'Kingston' comes from the town's Saxon name of Cyningestum, which meant the 'King's Estate'.

According to *The Anglo-Saxon Chronicle*, which was a contemporary account of events, there is no doubt that both Athelstan (*c.* 925–39) and Ethelred the Unready (978–1016) were crowned in Kingston. There is less certainty about the other kings named on the plinth: Edward the Elder (899–925), Edmund (939–46), Eadred (946–55), Edwy (955–59) and Edward the Martyr (975–78).

Kingston upon Thames has other royal connections. Elizabeth I founded Kingston Grammar School in 1561, and in 1628 Charles I granted a charter that allowed the town to hold the only market within a 7-mile (11-km) radius. The present bridge was built in 1825, replacing the old stone bridge, and was opened by the Duchess of Clarence, who was later to become Queen Adelaide.

ABOVE: *The Coronation Stone is believed to be the Anglo-Saxon stone on which several kings were crowned in Kingston-upon-Thames.*

HAMPTON COURT PALACE
Hampton, Middlesex

When Thomas Wolsey took out a lease on Hampton Court in 1514, he acquired a relatively modest building. However, his plans were far from modest, because not only was he highly ambitious in his career, but he also wanted to create one of the most splendid houses in Britain. He certainly succeeded in his aims, as he became a Cardinal and the Lord Chancellor in 1515, and his house gained the grandeur and opulence that matched his elevated position. Sadly for Wolsey, his status and eminence did not last. In 1528, he gave Hampton Court to Henry VIII in a vain attempt to appease the king who was incensed that Wolsey could not negotiate his divorce from Katherine of Aragon. Henry seized the house greedily, and had Wolsey imprisoned in the Tower of London (see page 55).

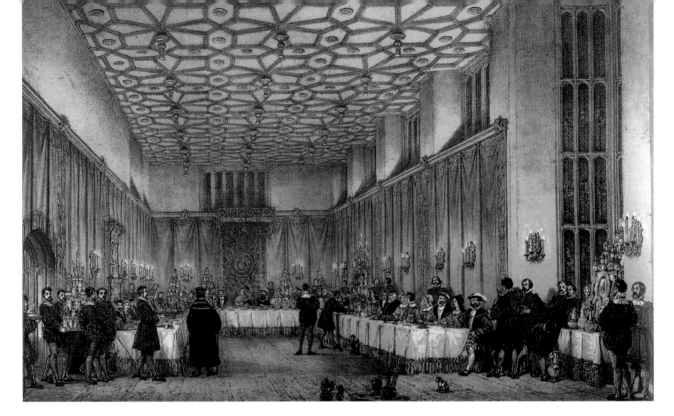

Henry at Hampton Court

Henry quickly set about turning Hampton Court into a royal palace. He loved the place, although it had unhappy memories for him because it was here in October 1537 that his third wife, Jane Seymour, died from complications after giving birth to the son he had craved for so long. In the autumn of 1541, Henry's fifth wife, Katherine Howard, was accused of adultery, a crime of high treason that was punishable by death. Ironically, Henry was given the news of her infidelity that November at Hampton Court, minutes after the couple had attended a thanksgiving service for their marriage. Katherine was confined to her rooms at the palace, but one day she managed to break free and ran along what is now called the Haunted Gallery to the door of the Chapel Royal, where Henry was attending a service. Before Katherine was able to reach the door she was captured by the guards and dragged back to her quarters. Legend has it that her ghost can still be seen and heard, rushing up and down the gallery and screaming. There is a curious coda to this story. In December 2003, it was announced that security cameras at the palace had picked up some ghostly activity, and clearly showed a figure in a cloak opening and shutting the doors in one of the exhibition areas. Although some of the guides at the palace wear period costume, none of

them wear anything like the clothes that were pictured on camera.

Hampton after Henry

After Henry VIII's death in 1547, Hampton Court continued to be a favourite royal palace, partly because Henry had created such a lavish set of buildings that they were the acme of comfort in what was often a very uncomfortable age. Although many of Henry's rooms were either demolished or altered during the modernizations carried out by Sir Christopher Wren at the behest of William and Mary in the 1690s, enough of them still stand to give a good idea of life at the Tudor court. For instance, Elizabeth I enjoyed attending elaborately produced plays in the Great Hall.

When James VI of Scotland succeeded to the throne of England in 1603 and became James I of England, he delighted in developing the surrounding land so he could enjoy his favourite sport of hunting. His son, Charles I, spent his honeymoon in the palace in 1625 and later commissioned ornamental lakes and ponds for the grounds. However, Hampton Court switched from being a palace to a prison during the English Civil War, when Charles was detained here on the orders of Oliver Cromwell in 1647. In the year of Charles I's execution, 1649, Parliament put Hampton Court on the open market, saying that the profits would be used to clear the royal debts and 'for the benefit of the Commonwealth'. The palace was sold in 1652 but bought back the following year, after Oliver Cromwell became Lord Protector. He moved into the palace with his family, and lived here until his death in 1658.

After the Restoration in 1660, Hampton Court once again became a royal palace, and Charles II busied himself trying to trace all the royal treasures that had been sold during the Civil War. Like his father, Charles spent his honeymoon at Hampton Court. However, he was hardly the most faithful husband and later installed various mistresses in lodgings on the estate, including Barbara Villiers, Lady Castlemaine (1641–1709).

When William and Mary came to the throne in 1689, they quickly commissioned Sir Christopher Wren to modernize Hampton Court. The original plan was to raze all the buildings, with the exception of the Tudor Great Hall, but a combination of Mary's early death and an ever-diminishing budget prevented such radical changes taking place. William was intimately involved in Wren's improvements, but he did not live long enough to enjoy them as he fell from his horse while out riding in Hampton Court Park in 1702, and died a short while afterwards.

The Last of Hampton Court's Kings
The first two Hanoverian kings were the last monarchs to live at Hampton Court. George I's court was considered to be very dull, but his son made up for that when he became king in 1727. George II brought his family here every summer, and commissioned William Kent to design the rooms now known as the Cumberland Suite for his second son, the Duke of Cumberland. George had no desire to build anything similar for his eldest son, Prince Frederick, whom he despised.

Hampton Court's life as a royal palace that housed the full court came to an abrupt end in 1737 when Queen Caroline, wife of George II, died. George continued to visit the palace, but never again with a full retinue. George III had no desire to live here and 40 members of staff were left to look after the palace.

RIGHT: *The Royal Arms of Henry VIII are carved on the panel above the massive doors of the central gateway of Hampton Court Palace.*

Gradually, the furniture and treasures were removed to other palaces, although these were later returned to Hampton Court during a long phase of restoration in the 19th century.

The palace survived the two World Wars almost unscathed, despite the number of bombs that rained down on London in the 1940s. However, it was not so lucky in March 1986 when a major fire broke out, causing an immense amount of damage to the King's Apartments. Restoration took six years but enabled the rooms to be returned to their 18th-century appearance. The restored King's Apartments were reopened by the Queen in July 1992. Ironically, a major fire broke out in Windsor Castle in November that same year, causing extensive damage. Many of the craftsmen who had worked with such care at Hampton Court were once again pressed into service at Windsor.

FURTHER READING

Arnold-Baker, Charles, *The Companion to British History*, Routledge, 2001

Bird, Charles, *Curiosities of London and Westminster*, S.B. Publications, 2003

Buckingham Palace, Royal Collection Enterprises, 2002

Clarence House, Royal Collection Enterprises, 2003

David, Saul, *Prince of Pleasure*, Little, Brown, 1998

Fraser, Antonia, *King Charles II*, Weidenfeld & Nicolson, 1979

Fraser, Antonia, ed., *The Lives of the Kings & Queens of England*, Weidenfeld & Nicolson, 1975

Glinert, Ed, *The London Compendium*, Allen Lane, 2003

Hampton Court Palace, Historic Royal Palaces, 2002

Hampton Court Palace, The King's Apartments, Historic Royal Palaces

Hibbert, Christopher, *London*, Penguin Books, 1980

Hilliam, David, *Crown, Orb and Sceptre*, Sutton, 2001

Hilliam, David, *Kings, Queens, Bones and Bastards*, Sutton, 1998

Humphreys, Rob, *The Rough Guide to London*, Rough Guides, 2003

Kensington Palace, Historic Royal Palaces, 2001

Impey, Edward and Parnell, Geoffrey, *The Tower of London*, Merrell Publishers, 2000

Lamont-Brown, Raymond, *Royal Poxes and Potions*, Sutton, 2001

Longford, Elizabeth, *The Oxford Book of Royal Anecdotes*, Oxford University Press, 1989

Panton, Kenneth, *London*, Tempus Publishing, 2001

Prochaska, Frank, *Royal Lives*, Oxford University Press, 2002

Robinson, John Martin, *Buckingham Palace*, Royal Collection Enterprises, 2000

Tames, Richard, *London*, The Windrush Press, 2002

The Banqueting House, Historic Royal Palaces, 2000

The Banqueting House in the Seventeenth Century, Historic Royal Palaces, 1996

The Tower of London, Historic Royal Palaces, 2002

Weinreb, Ben, and Hibbert, Christopher, ed., *The London Encyclopedia*, Macmillan Reference Books, 1995

Weir, Alison, *Britain's Royal Families*, The Bodley Head, 1989

Weir, Alison, *The Six Wives of Henry VIII*, The Bodley Head, 1991

Wittich, John, *Discovering London Curiosities*, Shire 1997

INDEX

ACKNOWLEDGEMENTS

I grew up listening to stories about London. They were told to me by my grandfather, father and mother, who all had a particular love and fascination for the City of London in which they worked. Later, when I lived in London, I became completely captivated by its romance and history, and the knowledge that reminders of its story were everywhere, from thought-provoking street names to medieval jetties above modern shop-fronts. So I was thrilled when Jo Hemmings at New Holland asked me to write this book. I would like to thank her for giving me the chance to write it, and also thank the rest of the New Holland team who worked on this book, especially my editors Camilla MacWhannell, Rose Hudson and Gareth Jones, for all their help and expertise. Many thanks, too, to Ricky Leaver for his wonderful photographs, and to Chelsey Fox and Bill Martin who, as ever, provided exactly the right support and encouragement.

All photographs by Ricky Leaver except for the following:

p14:   Dr. John Crook
p16:   The Royal Collection © 2005, Her Majesty Queen Elizabeth II
       (Photographer Derry Moore)
p56:   Crown ©/The Royal Collection © 2005, Her Majesty Queen Elizabeth II
p67:   Alberto Arzoz
p72:   Mary Evans Picture Library
p86:   British Library Picture Library
p109: National Maritime Museum
p117: Syon House